Praise for

MASTERS OF MODERN SOCCER

"Marrying first-rate reportage with stylish writing, Grant Wahl demonstrates why he's considered the dean of U.S. soccer writing —a master of modern soccer, so to speak. This book has the weight and depth to appeal to hardcores, and the smart analysis to captivate the casual fan. Soccer's answer to *Men at Work*."

—Jon Wertheim, *Sports Illustrated* executive editor

"Grant Wahl is a master of modern soccer writing and this book is a Rosetta stone for anyone who wants to fully understand the contemporary game. It's a user's manual to how the game is (or ought to be) played, coached, managed, and watched. Everyone interested in soccer—fans, youth coaches, even top professionals—will gain fascinating insights from some of the game's finest craftsmen, one of whom is Wahl himself."

—Steve Rushin, author of *Sting-Ray Afternoons* and columnist for *Sports Illustrated*

"I started it taking off at LAX and finished it landing at JFK. It's an incredible peek behind the curtain into the way players, coaches, and technical directors see themselves and their jobs. These entertaining and candid profiles help explain some of the complexities and mysteries of the beautiful game and the people who inhabit it."

—Alexi Lalas

ALSO BY GRANT WAHL

The Beckham Experiment

MASTERS OF MODERN SOCCER

HOW THE WORLD'S BEST
PLAY THE TWENTY-FIRST-CENTURY GAME

GRANT WAHL

THREE RIVERS PRESS
NEW YORK

Library of Congress Cataloging-in-Publication Data
Names: Wahl, Grant, author.
Title: Masters of Modern Soccer : How the World's Best Play the
Twenty-First-Century Game / Grant Wahl.
Description: First edition. | New York : Crown Archetype, [2018] |
Includes index.
Identifiers: LCCN 2017053620 | ISBN 9780307408600 |
ISBN 9780804137065 (eISBN)
Subjects: LCSH: Soccer. | Soccer players.
Classification: LCC GV943.W335 2018 | DDC 796.334—dc23 LC record
available at https://lccn.loc.gov/2017053620

ISBN 978-0-307-40861-7
Ebook ISBN 978-0-8041-3706-5

PRINTED IN THE UNITED STATES OF AMERICA

Book design: Andrea Lau
Illustrations: Andrea Lau
Cover design: Gregg Kulick
Cover photographs: (soccer player/background) Dmytro Aksonov/E+/Getty Images;
(soccer ball) TF-Images/Contributor/Getty Images

1 3 5 7 9 10 8 6 4 2

First Paperback Edition

Céline

CONTENTS

INTRODUCTION

WHEN DID I KNOW FOR SURE THAT I WAS GOING TO LOVE writing this book? The moment came early, on the first question of my first interview with Manchester City centerback Vincent Kompany. I had never met Kompany before, but I had admired him for years, and during my initial research for this book his name had come up repeatedly when I asked my journalist friends around Europe to nominate players who combined world-class talent and accomplishment with a high degree of intelligence and insight in interviews about the sport. My question was simple enough: What does the term *the modern game* mean to you?

Kompany considered the topic briefly and answered. "I think the term *modern football* just means that every single aspect of the game has improved," he said. "Players are quicker now. They try to play quicker and see the pass quicker. Players try to be more technical. Players *are* more physical. Maybe they're not tougher, because that sometimes has to do with their background, but the physical attitudes have definitely increased. So the modern game is all about an improved version of what it used to be."

What followed in that first interview was an hour-long discussion about the sport that left me exhilarated—and looking forward to more opportunities to speak to Kompany and the other figures in this book. The results of those interviews are in the following chapters. Everything they shared with me I will pass on to you.

It's easy to be cynical about modern soccer. For some observers, "the modern game" speaks mostly to the influence of money and commercialization on the sport, which is undeniable. To the critics, the apotheosis of modern soccer was probably the moment in July 2017 when the players of Manchester United and Real Madrid, on a promotional preseason tour in the United States, all high-fived a guy in a red-wigged Ronald McDonald costume before kickoff in an NFL stadium as though he were an actual player in the game. But over the two years of reporting for this book, my conversations with the seven practitioners in *Masters of Modern Soccer* overpowered any cynicism I might have had and gave me a heightened appreciation for the modern game—for the craft of the sport, position by position, and all the nuances that come with it. Kompany is right. Soccer is being played at a higher level than ever before, and by more players in more places than at any point in the history of the sport.

All the participants in this book give us an insider's view of soccer at the highest level, revealing how they experience and process the modern game. Manuel Neuer of Bayern Munich and the German national team explains how he redefined the goalkeeper position, making *sweeper keeper* part of the global soccer lexicon. Kompany, the Man City and Belgium veteran, shows why he is among today's shrinking group of world-class centerbacks, detailing the tricks of the trade for defenders in a time of high back lines and full-field pressure—as well as his decision making on when to push forward with the ball at his feet. Xabi Alonso, who won Champions League titles with Liverpool and Real Madrid and the World Cup with Spain, may be fond of the phrase *old school*, but his approach to the defensive midfield is decidedly modern. That includes his technical and positional mastery, his control of tempo, and his ability to change formations within the same game and tailor his own game to the needs of different teammates at different clubs. Christian Pulisic, the budding superstar attacking midfielder for the United States and Borussia Dortmund, speaks at length of his relentless pursuit of progress, his refusal to go sideways or backward, and his elemental desire to "break ankles" and beat defenders one-on-one. For his part, Mexican forward Javier "Chicharito" Hernández extols the virtues of constant movement in the penalty box and his desire to be a complete forward who does everything possible to be ready for the next game in a punishing modern schedule. Roberto Martínez, the Belgian national team coach, realizes the benefits of adaptation: to new playing styles, to new ways of thinking, and even to new countries—all while finding his own strong voice and making his teams better than the sum of their parts. And Borussia Dortmund sporting director Michael Zorc? All he did was respond to the near-bankruptcy of his hometown club by devising a strategy that sustained a new business model and allowed Dortmund to compete for trophies against rivals with far more money—a fact of life in modern soccer, which has no salary caps.

The modern game has more choreography than you might expect, and not just from set pieces, as we learn from the systematic patterns in the run of play used by Chicharito and the Mexican national team. And while there is less interchangeability of positions today than there was in the 1970s heyday of Total Football, the increasing *specialization* of positions in modern soccer requires a bigger skill set than it did in the past. It's not enough for a goalkeeper just to stop shots anymore; he also has to distribute the ball and cover the area outside the penalty box behind his high back line. It's not enough for a centerback to lock down the opposing striker; he also has to be a key figure starting the attack. It's not enough for a central midfielder to ping passes around; he has to be in the perfect position—not even two yards askance—or his team will be punished in a heartbeat on the counter. And it's not enough for a forward just to score goals anymore; he has to be the first harassing line of defense.

The specialization of the modern game extends to management as well. As I'll argue in the pages ahead, having a head coach to prepare the first team and a separate director of football to focus on long-term strategy and player acquisitions is a smart solution for the demands of the sport in the 21st century. Asking a traditional English-style manager to be responsible for all those tasks is asking for dysfunction.

The U.S. men's national team's failure to qualify for World Cup 2018 is a major setback, yet I hope it forces Americans to ask how this country can produce more incandescent talents like Pulisic. He is already America's best player as a teenager, and he holds his own with the veterans in this book when it comes to providing insight on how he views his position on the field.

Pulisic may well turn into the U.S.'s first men's global soccer superstar, and it was a thrill to spend time interviewing him as he improves at a breathtaking pace, almost by the week. In the 21st century, you can hail from anywhere on the planet—even Hershey, Pennsylvania—and become a master of modern soccer.

1

THE MIDFIELDERS

Christian Pulisic's Relentless Pursuit of Progress and Xabi Alonso's Mastery of Time and Space

IT'S AN UNDENIABLE FACT: THE UNITED STATES HAS NEVER produced a global men's soccer superstar. Have there been solid American players good enough to qualify for seven of the last eight World Cups? Sure. Mainstay goalkeepers who've enjoyed long careers in the English Premier League? No doubt. Even a rare top scorer for a midlevel European team? There's always Clint Dempsey and his 22 goals for Fulham in 2011–12. But for all the growth of soccer in America over the last two decades—in the popularity of the men's and women's World Cups, in the rise of domestic leagues, in media coverage of the planet's most popular sport—we have yet to find a U.S. men's version of The Chosen One. Which is to say, a true superstar, the best player on one of the top 10 clubs in the UEFA Champions League.

The reasons for this failure are many, we're told, and mostly related to culture. The majority of our best athletes go pro in other sports, from American football to basketball to baseball. Our most popular spectator sport, American football, is more about following orders than about the individual creativity we see in the best soccer players. Soccer is a pay-to-play, middle- to upper-middle-class pursuit in the United States, unlike in the rest of the world, where the working classes produce the best players with the drive to rise to the top of a Darwinian global pyramid. What's more, when it comes to youth soccer development, most experts will tell you the U.S. doesn't have nearly enough qualified coaches at the vital early ages—and that the coaches who are in place tend to value strength and athleticism over skills.

But there's another factor, too. The U.S. *has* produced teenage soccer players with the potential to be world class, but the all too common result has been prospects who thought they had "made it" by simply signing a healthy contract or joining a European club. Coddled by youth coaches and handlers, pumped up by the leagues, and showered with premature accolades by media and sponsors searching for the elusive American Soccer Savior (always that word, *savior*), these putative Chosen Ones decided they had climbed Mount Everest when all they had done was reach base camp. No example of the phenomenon is more sobering than that of Freddy Adu, who joined D.C. United at age 14 as the highest-paid player in Major League Soccer in 2004 and headlined a national television advertising campaign that year with Pelé. Though Adu showed flashes of talent for U.S. youth national teams, he never earned the trust of a coach at club level, where he played for 13 teams in 13 years, and was last seen riding the bench in the U.S. second division, a cautionary tale of blinding promise unfulfilled.

All of which brings us to a low-slung, redbrick residential building in a quiet neighborhood on the east side of Dortmund, a former steel-and-coal city in western Germany's Ruhr Valley. The two-story structure, fronted by evergreens and a small lawn, is the home of an American teenage soccer star, but it's conspicuous not for what it is, but rather for what it *isn't*. The place looks entirely ordinary from the outside. The windows—two rectangular slits on each floor—are usually covered by metal shades that give the building the appearance of a military bunker. The dead-end street is, well, pretty dead. There are industrial warehouses, a modest health club, the administrative office for a grocery store. All things considered, the tableau could just as well be a bland suburb of Pittsburgh.

And that's the whole point if you're Christian Pulisic, the 19-year-old Hershey, Pennsylvania, native who has emerged as one of the world's most promising attacking midfielders for Borussia Dortmund and the best prospect in the history of U.S. men's soccer. When Pulisic signed a new four-year contract in early 2017 and his father, Mark, moved back to the United States after two years in Germany, Christian could have decided he had arrived and splurged on his first adult apartment in one of the gorgeous new glass-and-steel buildings on Dortmund's Lake Phoenix, a bustling hub of bars, restaurants, and nightlife. Instead, he chose a street with no bars and no restaurants—and, truth be told, barely any neighbors at all—that's a five-minute drive from Dortmund's training facility.

That's not to say Pulisic's apartment is shabby inside. In fact, it's the dream dorm suite of any college freshman—which is exactly what Pulisic would be in the spring of 2018—if that freshman had ample amounts of discretionary income and a cleaning lady who came every week. "There's a lot of space, but nobody had lived in this building for three years," says Pulisic, welcoming me inside and giving me the grand tour two days before a game against Bayern Munich. Pulisic is renting, not buying, but he got permission from the owner to spruce up an indoor swimming pool on the ground floor with colorful tile work on the wall and a poolside hangout area. Upstairs, the main living room has enough space to toss 20-yard passes with an American football and features a pool table, a folded-up ping-pong table, and a big-screen TV for watching soccer, NFL, and NBA games. The walls are filled mostly with blown-up photographs of Dortmund's Signal Iduna Park, Germany's largest stadium, where more than 81,000 adoring fans cheer on their team in a roiling sea of black and yellow.

Once again: Think Pittsburgh. "You go out into the city and you just see black and yellow everywhere," says Pulisic. "They're wearing jerseys, jackets. I've never seen a town that's so connected and so proud of their team and so passionate about the game. That's what makes Dortmund stand out so much. The weather isn't very good, but it's just a great town to live in. It's really known for the soccer."

Pulisic has thick eyebrows, a ready smile, and, now that he has graduated from adolescence into adulthood, a chiseled chin and cheekbones; if there's ever a movie made about his life, he might be played by the actor Jake Gyllenhaal. In Germany, everyone pronounces Pulisic's last name *POOL-uh-sitch*, the way it would be in Croatia, the birthplace of his grandfather Mate. That lineage allowed Christian to acquire a Croatian passport and start playing for Dortmund at age 16, earlier than he would have been able to with his U.S. citizenship alone. When he's in the United States, Pulisic asks people to pronounce his name the Americanized way: *puh-LISS-ick*.

Pulisic realizes he hasn't made it to the pinnacle yet just because he got to this point in his career. He has to do more. With the maturity of someone 10 years older, he's studying the craft of an attacking midfielder. "Now that I'm at a higher level and playing in the Bundesliga, you think of it more as your job," Pulisic says. "How can I become the best? How can I take a certain aspect of the game and improve that to make myself better overall? Of course, we play because we always love the game. But it's about figuring out what you need to take that next step. That's what I think about now."

In a case of perfect symmetry, Pulisic's bedrock philosophy—a relentless pursuit of progress—also applies to how he plays his position on the field. Whether he's starting out wide (as he often does at Dortmund) or centrally (as he does more regularly for the United States), Pulisic has a visceral distaste for touches or passes that go sideways or backward. "My coaches taught me a lot is about taking the first touch positive, and I think that's what I've tried to base my game off of," he explains. "A big part of it is being aggressive. It's not just about getting the ball and figuring out every time how you can keep possession, because there are plenty of players who can do that. That's just not how I view my performances. It's about: What can I do to change the game and the attacking aspect of the game? That's how I look at it every time. Every single play is just doing what you can to keep your defender off balance so he has no idea what's coming next. It's being positive and going towards the goal because that's my position. I'm an *attacking* midfielder."

The last four years of Pulisic's life are a study in constant transformation. He moved first from his home in Pennsylvania to the U.S. Under-17 national team residency program in Bradenton, Florida; then to Dortmund to live with his father; and then into his own adult apartment. He graduated from Dortmund's Under-17 team to its Under-19 team to its first team. He grew, physically and emotionally, from a child to a man. If you Google "2013 Nike Friendlies" and watch the highlights of Pulisic's U.S. Under-17 team beating Brazil 4–1—the day he realized he could compete against anyone in the world—you'll see a talented but still callow 15-year-old boy.

Of all the things that have changed for Pulisic, however, at least one surprising aspect has not. "The funny thing is I've worn the same cleat size for the last, like, four years," he says. "I feel like my foot has definitely grown, but I haven't done anything about it." Pulisic wears U.S. size 8.5 soccer cleats—the Nike Mercurial Vapor, his standbys since 2011—that are a full size smaller than his running shoes (size 9.5). Yet his cleats aren't painful to wear, he says. *He wants them that way.* "You just feel like your foot is closer to the ball, like you have more control over it," Pulisic explains. "If you have a big gap between your toe and the edge of your shoe, I feel like it's not nearly as comfortable when you're touching the ball."

The first touch is the foundation of an attacking midfielder's relationship with the ball. You have to learn how to control the ball with your feet, as if they were hands, supple and cushioning, welcoming passes of varying weights without a second thought and setting up your next action. The task of a first touch becomes harder when you're under the pressure of an advancing defender. One easy way to tell the difference in the levels of professional players—and teams and leagues, for that matter—is in the quality of their first touches. If the ball clangs off players' feet and legs with any regularity, you're probably not watching a Champions League knockout game.

The knock on American players is that their first touch isn't, shall we say, cultured. During the 2016 Copa América Centenario, one snarky fan went so far as to post a YouTube compilation video—set to European trance music, like so many soccer highlight videos—of the U.S. forward Gyasi Zardes butchering first touches and losing possession of the ball. To his credit, Zardes has enough speed, determination, and finishing ability to at least partially make up for his control flaws, especially as an MLS player, but, at his age (26) as a professional, it's impossible to perfect a first touch. Like so many other technical skills, it is best learned between the ages of three and nine, not 10 or 20 years later.

Pulisic, for his part, began working on his first touch at an early age with his father, Mark, who was a professional soccer player and is now a coach. "It starts when I'm five years old," Christian says, "and my dad's punting the ball in the air and I'm just bringing it down and working on my first touch with both feet." Mark emphasizes that he wanted sports—including sports other than soccer—to be fun for Christian at that age, but that didn't prevent the youngster from learning the fundamentals.

First-touch work continues for Borussia Dortmund's youth and senior teams in regular practice sessions and on the Footbonaut, a $3.5 million machine pioneered by the club that has its own building at the team's training ground. (Mark Pulisic oversaw the Footbonaut during his two years as a Dortmund youth team coach.) The Footbonaut takes Teutonic efficiency to its *fußball* extremes. Built as an apartment-sized, cube-shaped cage, the machine fires balls from a range of 360 degrees at different speeds and trajectories toward the player, who then has to control the ball with his first touch, raise his head to spot the destination (an electronically lit-up square on the perimeter), and pass the ball into the target. Coaches dial up the speed and reps and keep score of the participants' success rate. Sometimes they add a defender to mark the player in the center circle.

In a game situation, the first touch is never an end in itself. "As you get older, it's about the movements," Pulisic says. "It's knowing which direction to take your first touch, and not just receiving it. A lot of times it's not about stopping the ball under your foot and not having any options after that. It's putting yourself in a good position for what you want to do with it." Pulisic, in particular, has a talent for using his first touch as an attacking weapon to slice through defenses. As his teammate Nuri Şahin says, "He's fearless. He has so much speed, but what I like the most is his first touch. When he gets the ball, his first touch opens him a huge space even if there is no space."

The ability to use space—finding it, creating it, exploiting it—is the hallmark of the modern attacking midfielder. No player in the history of the game did more to innovate the position than the Dutch legend Johan Cruyff, who had mastered the technical aspects of the game at such a young age that he focused thereafter on the tactical side: positioning, movement, and speed, always with coordinated teamwork. With Cruyff, simplicity and efficiency were paramount, both on and off the ball. He had no time for attacking midfielders (or any players, for that matter) who were not fully engaged in the game for 90 minutes, the vast majority of that time spent away from the ball. Cruyff's creativity had elements of genius, so it wasn't always repeatable as a craft, but he also had trademark moves—like the Cruyff Turn, in which he evaded a defender by tapping the ball behind his plant foot, turning and moving in a different direction—that were copied around the world. Cruyff was a transformational figure, both as a player and as a manager, and his attacking philosophies in the 1970s and '80s at Ajax and Barcelona continue to have a clear influence on the game today. "Quality without results is pointless," he famously said. "Results without quality is boring."

So much of modern soccer is about utilizing space and pressure. Pulisic has learned that he can't take an attacking first touch all the time. If he's in a central position deeper on the field, he says, he'll sometimes be more conservative and hold the ball, not least because losing it in your own end can quickly lead to a goal by the other team. But if he's higher up the field, his attack-first mentality is fully engaged, whether Dortmund has advanced the ball from its own half or has won the ball in the opposing end using its notorious defensive pressure. Dortmund's pressing requires every player, including forwards and attacking midfielders like Pulisic, to work together in unison. If one player slacks off, the pressure fizzles. The commitment is exhausting and requires peak fitness and concentration, but the rewards can be enormous.

In transitions, the team that has just lost the ball is often unbalanced and exposed. It's up to Pulisic and his teammates to take advantage of the opening as soon as possible. "When my team wins the ball or when I win the ball, your first look always goes forward," Pulisic says. "That's something our coach here in Dortmund [Thomas Tuchel at the time] stresses a lot. You don't know: Someone could be peeling off and making a run forward, and you can slip a ball in. Anytime you can get to the goal as quick as you can, it catches the other team off guard, especially when they've just lost the ball." On the other hand, when Dortmund loses the ball, Pulisic has to make a decision in defensive transition. If he's close to the ball, he says, he'll put pressure on the ball carrier. If he's farther away, he'll retreat to defend a space. That's modern soccer: Even as an attacking midfielder, Pulisic will always have defensive responsibilities. His attention to defense has helped earn him minutes on the field.

If you listen to Pulisic describe what he's thinking about during a game as he plays the position of attacking midfielder, the word he uses most often is *next*. Like a chess grandmaster, he's always anticipating the moves ahead. It reminded me of Bora Milutinović, the peripatetic Serb who has coached five different countries in the World Cup. Soon after Bora took over the U.S. team ahead of the 1994 tournament, he posed a riddle to his players: What is the most important play? They were all stumped at first. When I visited China in 2002 to write a *Sports Illustrated* story on Bora's Chinese men's team, which had qualified for its first (and still only) World Cup, the players said the coach asked the same question. "At first nobody knew," said Yu Huixian, Bora's interpreter. "A goal? A good pass? Defensive pressure? Bora finally had to explain it to them." Later I asked winger Qu Bo: What is the most important play? "Everyone knows the answer to that," he said, laughing. "It's the *next* play."

When Pulisic wants to pass the ball to a teammate, he takes into account several factors, chief among them what the player will do upon receiving the ball. "A lot of things go into it," Pulisic says. "It's the weight of the pass. It's which foot you're passing it to and which side of his body so that he can take it into a positive area. So it's a lot of thinking about what he has to do with the ball *next*. And then it's all about the direction and speed of the pass. There are so many types of passes that are about weight, and that's what some of the best number sixes [deep-lying midfielders] in the world are great at: They can just ping [the ball] across the field and hit it on a dime on the guy's left foot. That's a skill I'm definitely trying to develop, but I'm not there yet."

One aspect of Pulisic's game in which he has nearly reached full maturity is beating defenders one-on-one with the ball. Witnessing him perform the soccer equivalent of "breaking ankles" on a basketball court and whoosh past seasoned European pros with a combination of speed, guile, and raw explosive power is a rush of pure adrenaline for anyone who's watching in the stadium or on TV. You're left with a slack-jawed sense of wonder: *Did an American teenager just do that?* In Pulisic's confidence on the field and even in his appearance—maybe it's that high-and-tight haircut—he's a postmillennial version of Tom Cruise's Maverick taking out the MiGs in *Top Gun*. You half-expect Pulisic to wear a bomber jacket, drive a motorcycle, and play beach volleyball bare-chested in jeans in his spare time.

When Pulisic has the ball and advances on a defender from a wide position, his head is up and he's observing his foe, processing what he sees millisecond by millisecond. "A lot of times you see which way he's forcing you and which way his body's turned," Pulisic says. "If you can get him to swivel his hips and wrong-foot him, that's the first step in taking someone on. You want to move the ball side to side and see what he's going to do with it. Once he starts moving and switching sides, that's when you have him. Use your pace and change direction and *go*." Should Pulisic stay out wide or cut inside? Sometimes he knows what he'll do from the moment he receives the ball. On other occasions, his decision depends on the defender. "If he's giving you enough space to the inside and he's cutting off that endline because he doesn't want you to play a ball in, then you take it inside and explode by him," Pulisic explains. "When I'm playing, I'm not even really thinking about it. It kind of feels natural when you start going at him. It almost seems like he's telling you to go one way."

Yet Pulisic doesn't want to be too predictable in one-on-one situations. Like a baseball pitcher, he'll keep a defender guessing by mixing up his speeds. First, Pulisic might cut inside and turn on the jets. But when his opponent tries to catch up, Pulisic will stop in his tracks as his hapless foil overpursues and Pulisic moves in a different direction, the bamboozle complete. Unlike a baseball pitcher, Pulisic can also disguise his intent by being dangerous using both feet. He's naturally right-footed, and he says he would shoot a free kick or a penalty with his right foot. If he has a lot of space and a simple shot that he needs to hit with power, he'll probably go with his right peg. But he won't change the direction of his movement to favor his right foot, he says. That's why he has spent so much time improving his left foot since he started working on it with his father as a five-year-old. "Every day in training, even if it's just a simple passing drill, I try to do as many with my left as I do with my right," Pulisic says.

Yes, it's possible to be so lethal on one dominant foot that you can still thrive by moving exactly where everyone expects you to go: Arjen Robben has built a long career on cutting in on his left foot from the right wing for Bayern Munich and the Netherlands. Nor have Lionel Messi and Diego Maradona been hindered by their pedestrian right feet, a weakness that's mitigated when their left feet are historic repositories of physical genius. But those men are outliers, in Pulisic's opinion. "I think it just helps so much when you have two options [right and left feet] that are just as strong," he says, which means defenders can't shade him to go in one direction.

Ultimately, beating his opponents one-on-one in the attacking third of the field is one of the clearest ways Pulisic can fulfill his objectives and change the game. Even if he's successful, more work remains to be done, whether it's through a continuation of his run, a cross (if he's out wide), a through-ball (if he's more central), or a shot on goal. And if Pulisic isn't successful taking on his defender *mano a mano*? Well, that's just part of the game. You can't be afraid to take risks in that part of the field. "If I go at a defender and lose it," Pulisic says, "I'm not going to hear something from my coach because I tried to take him on in that side of the field. If you can take down that one player, you free yourself up and the whole game is open in that final third." Truth be told, Pulisic's toughest audience isn't his coach or his teammates or the thousands of fans in the stands. It's himself. He competes at such a revved-up intensity that when he makes a mistake—and even the best soccer players commit plenty of errors—his visceral reaction is plain for everyone in the stadium to see. Pulisic says that whenever his frustration builds after losing two or three balls in a row, he tries to restore his confidence as quickly as possible by making a simple pass to a teammate. Oftentimes, that's all he needs to get back at it.

Managing his emotions on the field can have positive consequences. During a play in the U.S.'s 2017 home World Cup qualifier against Honduras, Pulisic runs onto the ball just outside the top of the opposing penalty box and tries to beat a defender but fails. Instead of shutting down, though, he stays engaged.

Teammate Jozy Altidore recovers the ball and hits a gorgeous through-ball to Pulisic. His shot is saved, but Sebastian Lletget pounces on the rebound for a tap-in goal. USA 1, Honduras 0. "When you lose a ball in a dangerous area like that, especially when you have numbers, you can't just put your head down and walk off," Pulisic says. "Because the play's definitely not over. You don't know what could happen. And just like that Jozy gave me a perfect ball there."

A funny thing happens as we watch video together from a wide range of Pulisic's games for both Dortmund and the U.S. national team. They're in no chronological order, just a random collection of clips, and yet within a split second he's able to see an image and recall all the circumstances surrounding the play, including the opposing team and the context of the situation. Finally, I ask: "Do you have a photographic memory or something?"

"Every play I remember," Pulisic says. "You could show me any play. I'd probably know it." And there are so many "wow" moments that make Pulisic special, that demonstrate he's already one of the most promising attacking midfielders in the world.

Wow Moment Number 1: The time in March 2017 when Pulisic made something out of nothing to give the United States a 1–0 lead at a World Cup qualifier in Panama. U.S. midfielder Jermaine Jones sends a harmless-looking longball down the right side that appears to be corralled by the hulking Panamanian centerback Felipe Baloy at the edge of his penalty box. Pulisic, conceding four inches and 50 pounds to Baloy, is floating behind him like a wraith. From the opening whistle, Panama has targeted Pulisic, hacking him regularly, trying to bludgeon him out of the game. The Mexican referee, César Ramos, has done nothing to put a stop to the thuggery.

But now Pulisic strikes back. Baloy takes a heavy touch. Pulisic sneaks under his arm, retrieves the ball, and steps past the veteran defender's lunge in the box. Baloy's tag-team partner, the equally burly Román Torres, races over to stop Pulisic, who slides the ball over to his right foot, dribbles to the edge of the six-yard box, and ... stops cold in his tracks, right there in the penalty box. *Bamboozle engaged.* Torres overpursues, looking like Wile E. Coyote in that desperate moment when he has run past the edge of the cliff and is frozen in midair before falling to the canyon floor. Meanwhile, Pulisic has already seen Clint Dempsey flashing unmarked into the box. The hard work has already been done. The teenager lays off the ball for Dempsey's easy finish.

"It's one of my favorite plays," says Pulisic, who posted a photograph of Dempsey, finger pointed, running toward him in celebration of the goal as the wallpaper on his Twitter profile. "Once [Baloy] had control of the ball, it looked like he thought I had no chance at it, so he could just body me right off. But I didn't give up on the play, and once I got under his arm I saw the opportunity open up in the middle. As I was going at [Torres], right after my first touch I already knew I was going to pass it in to Clint, because I heard him yell and I saw the run out of the corner of my eye. I took him to the right because I knew I had to clear up some space, and then I cut it right back and laid it off for him. And you know Clint's going to score from there." The word that comes to mind watching Pulisic on the play is *poise*. Soccer can be a frenetic sport, especially in the penalty box, where scoring chances come and go in an instant and some of the world's best strikers can lose their nerve. But here Pulisic has the cojones to literally stop in the box with a defender draped over him. It's as if the game is unfolding at a slower speed for just one player on the field.

Wow Moment Number 2: The time Pulisic shredded the Honduran defense with assists on two more Dempsey goals in their March 2017 World Cup qualifier. On the first one, Pulisic (playing in a central midfield role) carries the ball at speed 40 yards from the goal with four Honduran defenders facing him, including one (captain Maynor Figueroa) directly in front of Pulisic. To his left, Dempsey darts toward the goal, making a run on the inside shoulder of his defender. "I know Jozy [Altidore] is to my right," Pulisic says, stopping the video at different times, "and I feel like Clint is making such a perfect run here that I can't leave him hanging, because he's in the best position on the field to score by far. I can dribble [Figueroa] to the right, no problem, but where does that really bring me? He's right in front of me, so I can go through his legs with a pass, but I felt like the lob was the best option for that specific play."

Using his right foot like a sand wedge, Pulisic lifts a delicate chip on the run over Figueroa that falls like a baby's breath onto Dempsey's right shoulder, and the Texan does the rest, bulling his way into the box to slam the ball into the upper-right corner of the goal. 3–0.

Later in the same game, Honduras makes an unforced giveaway in midfield, and the U.S. transition is on. With the opposing defense unbalanced, Altidore carries the ball down the left side past the halfway line. Pulisic, unmarked and running in parallel 10 yards away, calls for the ball with his arms outstretched toward the ground, like an airport worker directing a 747 into the right gate. Altidore delivers the pass to Pulisic, who then does something small that makes a giant difference. "I think I took a quick look," Pulisic recalls. "It's like a second before I receive the ball." We watch the play. *"There!"* That photographic memory again. *While Altidore's pass is traveling the 10 yards toward him,* the running Pulisic flashes his head a quarter-turn away from the approaching ball. It's enough for him to spot Dempsey charging down the middle, splitting the giant gap between two retreating Honduran defenders.

Pulisic says he takes "little snapshots" like this all the time. "Before you receive the pass, it's just taking looks around," he explains. "A great example of it is [Barcelona midfield greats] Xavi and [Andrés] Iniesta. Before they even receive a pass, they know everything that's around them. If you know what's around you when the ball is at your feet, then you don't even need to turn and see. You know which way to turn. You know which direction you're going. You know if there's a guy coming from your right or left if you're taking quick little snapshots."

As a result, Pulisic knows exactly what he wants to do—what comes *next*—before Altidore's pass arrives. "Now it's all about the weight of my pass [to Dempsey]," Pulisic says. "I know where it's going because there's a huge gap between those two defenders." If Pulisic delivers the pass too softly, he won't hit Dempsey in stride, and the advantage will be lost. If the pass is too strong, either the goalkeeper will reach the ball before Dempsey does or the path will take Dempsey into a shooting angle that's too tight. In the blink of an eye, Pulisic computes all the variables and, just before Honduras's Jorge Claros dives into him from the side on a tackle, sends a pass that's right on the money. "The weight was . . . it was one of the best passes I've made," Pulisic says. Dempsey does the rest, taking one touch before finishing the second of his three goals in the 6–0 blowout.

In real time, the sequence happens so fast. Only five seconds elapse from the time Altidore first touches the ball to the instant Pulisic hits his pass to Dempsey. But those five seconds contain multitudes. *Transition. Head up. Look downfield. Snapshot. First touch. What's next? Deliver a pass with the right weight and direction.* With all the talk of snapshots and a photographic memory, it's tempting to compare Pulisic to a fancy camera. But that would be underselling him. He's nothing less than a soccer supercomputer.

It's worth noting that Pulisic first wore the number 10 jersey for the United States at the remarkably young age of 17 on September 2, 2016 in a World Cup qualifying victory against St. Vincent and the Grenadines, in which he scored two goals. He may not give up that number for many, many years.

The number 10 is a mythical signifier in the sport, a symbol traditionally of the team's best player, the one with the biggest influence on the game. But apart from the actual digits on the back of a shirt, the number 10 is also a position, a particular type of attacking midfielder: the playmaker, the central hub of the offense. The gold standard for the number 10 position is Argentine legend Diego Maradona, whose creative genius—in his passing, his dribbling, and his scoring ability—was of such a level that it could be described not as modern but rather as timeless. One hopes there will always be a place in soccer for playmaking genius (Lionel Messi fits that description), but there are fewer "pure" number 10s in the sport today, perhaps because managers now are asking every player on the field to provide something in the way of defending.

The fact that Pulisic has become the U.S.'s main offensive threat means his attacking midfield role is different from the one he has at Dortmund, where he's important but not viewed as the team's best player. What's more, he often shoulders the responsibility of the number 10 position for the United States at a time when he's mainly being used on the wing or pinched in as part of the "2" of a 3-4-2-1 formation for Dortmund. In September 2017, then U.S. coach Bruce Arena revealed that he gives Pulisic the freedom to go anywhere on the field for the United States—a remarkable thing for a teenager on a national team. "When I go with the national team, especially in a number 10 position underneath big strikers in the style that we play, I feel like I'm asked a lot more to provide for [the strikers] and really connect the game and make a much bigger impact," Pulisic says. When Pulisic is with Dortmund, where the expectations of him are high but not the same, he wears the very complimentary number 22.

Wow Moment Number 3: In March 2017 Pulisic scored the decisive goal that sent Dortmund to the Champions League quarterfinals. Deadlocked at 1–1 on aggregate in the return leg at home against Portugal's Benfica, Dortmund has to break down a packed defense in the 59th minute in front of an 80,000-plus crowd. Ten Benfica players are behind the ball, which is held by right back Łukasz Piszczek 35 yards out from goal. Benfica has five defenders even with the front edge of the penalty box in its restraining line—the line past which Dortmund attackers would be offside—and two black-and-yellow players (Pierre-Emerick Aubameyang and Ousmane Dembélé) are central just inside the box.

How does Dortmund find an opening? Pulisic, starting at the top of the box, runs sideways across Benfica's back line toward the space where there's a gap between the centerback and the left back. Piszczek sees the run, and with no close defensive pressure on him he has time to pump-fake like an NFL quarter-back and act like he's hitting a ball in the air toward the attack-ers in the box. Instead, he passes on the ground toward Pulisic, who cuts hard to his left into the gap. At this point, Pulisic's head is still facing to the right, although the goal is to his left, his blind side. By the time Pulisic runs onto the ball 10 yards out from goal, goalkeeper Ederson is already bearing down on him to cut down the angle. But Pulisic has just enough time to chip the ball over Ederson and watch the slow-moving parabola arcing-arcing-arcing *just* under the crossbar. The stadium's Yel-low Wall—the largest freestanding grandstand in Europe, with space for 25,000 fans—erupts. It's Pulisic's first Champions League goal, and Dortmund won't fashion a more important one all season.

"I scored a goal identical to this in a friendly over winter break against a team from Belgium [Standard Liège]," Pulisic says, "and Piszczek was on the ball exactly like this." When I find the video of the previous goal later online, I'm dumbfounded. The sequence is *exactly* the same: the same Piszczek location and pass, the same Pulisic location and run; the same gap in the defense; the same Pulisic chip over an onrushing goalkeeper to finish. Photographic memory is one thing; photographic *repro-duction* is another. "I made a run straight across the back four," Pulisic says of the Benfica goal. "That's a really good pass from him to see that run. I know where the goal is. I don't know where the keeper is until my last three steps. Then all I see is him fly-ing out, and that's why I went with the chip. Because if he's flying out at you he's not going to go high, he's going to go down low. When I hit this chip, I thought I had missed it high." Only as Pulisic is crashing to the ground after being clipped by the goalkeeper does he see the ball strike the back of the net, punch his right fist in the air, and run for his trademark celebratory knee slide.

Going back to the first time I interviewed Pulisic, when he was 17 in February 2016, I have found him to be refreshingly introspective and thoughtful for a teenage athlete. When I returned to Dortmund to speak to him in October 2016, alongside a crew from Fox Sports television, Pulisic spoke about how he was still adjusting to being recognized in the streets and the realization that his mere presence somewhere could cause fans of varying ages to be overcome with excitement. He wasn't bothered by it, but he was possessed of a sense of wonder at the workings of celebrity culture. When I visit Pulisic again in Germany in April 2017, it's clear that while he's a natural performer on the soccer field, he's also well aware that his instincts aren't the same away from the stadium.

At one point I ask Pulisic: "In what ways do you think your personality is reflected in the way you play the attacking midfield position?"

"I don't think it is at all," he replies.

"Is that difference in any way interesting to you?"

He nods. "I consider myself more of a shy guy," he says. "When I'm with my friends, it can be different. But I'm not really the most outgoing person who wants to put myself out there. It's just how I grew up. My parents always taught me to be humble. But once you're on the field, you want *everyone* to know that you're the most confident guy out there and you're willing to do anything. That's just how I've always gone about it."

How much can a teenager know about the sport of soccer? More than you might think.

● ● ●

FORMER DEFENSIVE MIDFIELDER XABI ALONSO says he learned almost nothing new about how to pass the ball after he was an 18-year-old at Real Sociedad in La Liga. A natural distributor, Alonso was always able to hit any type of pass, from short *tiki-taka* touches to piercing through-balls on the counter-attack to 40-yard diagonal Hollywood passes. "That's never been the hard part for me," Alonso says. "But maybe I couldn't position myself as well" during his teenage years as he could later in his career.

Alonso is soccer's answer to George Clooney, a midfielder so cool and self-assured that you could imagine him playing the game in a tuxedo, perhaps while carrying a gin and tonic. *Desperation* is anathema to Alonso, which is why he thinks the elaborate midfield slide tackle—that bastion of English-style bustling commitment—is overrated. For what is a slide tackle, Alonso reasons, if not an admission that your positioning could have been better? "Especially in the U.K., some people understand—and some people don't," says the Basque Spaniard who played for such storied clubs as Liverpool, Real Madrid, and Bayern Munich in a 17-year pro career that ended in 2017, when he was 35. "If you are too much on the ground, then something is not right. I love good tackling, but I prefer the player who does not need to do that."

With an almost unmatched understanding of the game, Alonso was one of the defining defensive midfielders of his generation. He worked under some of the sport's premier managers—Carlo Ancelotti, Vicente del Bosque, José Mourinho, Rafa Benítez—but in 2014 he joined Bayern Munich with the intention of preparing for his *own* coaching career by immersing himself in the methods of Pep Guardiola. "I learned a lot those two years," says Alonso. "[It was] very useful for me to understand more about football and how I want to do things."

Wearing a black Mr. Rogers–style cardigan over a plain gray T-shirt, Alonso settles into a meeting room at Bayern's training ground and unpacks the duties of his position, which could be variously called a defensive midfielder or a "number six." If Pulisic can afford to prioritize his offense and creativity as an attacking midfielder, Alonso's role as a defensive midfielder required him to find a more equitable balance, leaning toward defense if there was ever any doubt. "You cannot relax; you have to be always on your toes," Alonso says. "It's not like a striker; they can afford 30 seconds [of rest] when they aren't involved. Midfielders have to be fully concentrated during the 90 minutes to be in the right place." Alonso is obsessed with positioning, movement, and space. That location education continued well into his 30s, accelerated at Bayern by studying Guardiola's constantly shape-shifting tactical approaches.

Did Alonso touch the ball a lot during his playing days? You'd better believe it. Using Opta's statistical database, the analyst Ben Torvaney found that during Alonso's first two seasons at Bayern Munich, he racked up the most passes completed of anyone on the team, making 112 per 90 minutes in 2014–15 and 98 per 90 in 2015–16. That value dropped down to a still-impressive 86 passes per 90 minutes in 2016–17, reflecting the change in the style of the team under new manager Carlo Ancelotti. The data also support Alonso's ability to adapt his style, depending on the situation. In his first season after joining Bayern, he made 17.7 long passes into the opposition half per 90 minutes,

the most of any player over a season during his three years at
Bayern. However, this value dropped down to 12.8 long passes
into the opposition half per 90 minutes in both 2015–16 and
2016–17. Being able to cultivate new ideas, like the importance
of short passing to maintain team shape, and incorporate them
into each game is part of what allows a player like Alonso to
keep playing at the highest level until the end of his career.

All things considered, Alonso's outsized influence on a match
was less about making killer passes than about controlling the
play through a critical mass of small choices—thousands of
them, 90 minutes at a time. These choices are the essence of a
defensive midfielder. "It's all about balance, about making a lot
of right decisions," Alonso says. "Maybe they look unmeaning-
ful [individually], but putting all of them together, they make
sense. My job is not to make spectacular actions. Maybe that
happens once in a while, but that's not my job."

The variety of attacking methods on Alonso's teams over
the years was remarkable. His Liverpool team won the 2005
Champions League crown with a dynamic quick-strike capabil-
ity that employed Steven Gerrard at the height of his powers.
When Spain won World Cup 2010, it suffocated opponents like
a python with short passes and maximum possession. Alonso's
Real Madrid raised the 2014 Champions League trophy largely
by funneling the ball to the ultimate avatar of whooshing athleticism, Cristiano Ronaldo. During the final three seasons of
Alonso's career, at Bayern Munich, his teams combined ball control with the ability to pounce on the break.

"During my years in Liverpool and Madrid, we didn't have as
much control with the passes as we do at Bayern," Alonso says.
"At Bayern we have much more ball possession. Many games I

make more than 100 passes. In Madrid and Liverpool we were more direct. I made fewer passes and had a lower completion rate, but it was more vertical. The buildup of the game was different. In Madrid I was playing with [Gareth] Bale, Cristiano [Ronaldo], Karim [Benzema], Mesut [Özil], and [Ángel] Di María. They like to run, so you need to take a little bit more risk. At Bayern we have more happening in the middle, so it's more about short passes, and sometimes you hit the long pass. Of course, my game and my passes are different and depend on the players around me. With Spain, when we were playing with [Sergio] Busquets, [Andrés] Iniesta, [David] Silva, and Xavi, we had so many passes. Most of them were short."

Each approach was different, yet Alonso's basic role when his team owned possession stayed the same. "When we win the ball, my job is to get it from the defense to the attackers in the best possible way," he says, "[so they can] go one-on-one or have a good position to make the last pass. You won't see me like [Real Madrid midfielder] Luka Modrić, dribbling *through* guys. That's hard for me. The pass—that is more natural for me."

Before Alonso could deliver a pass, though, he had to *receive* the ball. And before he could receive the ball, he had to be aware of what was surrounding him from a 360-degree perspective. The only way to do that was by constantly swiveling his head and employing his peripheral vision to register players (team-mates and opponents) and open space.

"I have never seen a [video] for the full 90 minutes, just on me," he says, "but I would be curious to see if I am always"—here he pantomimes darting his gaze in different directions, like a quarterback scanning the defensive secondary. His perspective calls to mind the 2006 documentary film *Zidane: A 21st Century*

Portrait, in which 17 synchronized cameras follow the legendary French midfielder Zinédine Zidane during the 90 minutes of a Real Madrid game. One thing that stands out in that film is how much time Zidane spends glancing around to understand where the space is—and where it isn't. "He was like a ballet dancer playing football," Alonso says, "like [Roger] Federer playing tennis. It was a joy to watch him. The most elegant player I've ever seen."

In modern soccer, defenders close down space in an instant, all over the field, which is why you have to map out the surrounding terrain in your mind's eye before they bear down on you. "Before receiving the pass, I try to have an idea of what's going to be the next decision," Alonso says. "When you get the ball, it's probably too late, because you will have the opponent on top of you."

When we watch video together of his games, more than once Alonso will freeze the screen and note that his head is turned away from the ball, scanning his surroundings, even though the ball is being passed to him at that very moment. In Alonso's opinion, too many professional midfielders make the mistake of ball watching. We all have an image in our heads of five-year-olds playing soccer and glomming onto the ball in a pack, kicking up a dust cloud like Pigpen in *Peanuts*, each of the children straining with all their might to kick the sphere. But Alonso says even pro midfielders, while not herding around the ball, are often guilty of moving too near to it. "When you get too close to your teammate, you don't gain any space for yourself once you receive the pass," he says. "So sometimes to run *less* is better, in my position. It is one of the basics of the midfielder. You don't have to go to the ball. The ball has to come to you. Then you know where the ball has to go. Because if you go too close, you are probably not in the right position to make that next pass. That's something that you learn with the games and the years."

As Pulisic grows older and gains more experience, he will understand more of what Alonso picked up over his 17-year career: As is the case with experience in any field, you learn not just what you need to do to succeed, but also what you *don't* need to do. The smarter your positioning is on the field, the less you'll have to run and the more efficient you'll be. Alonso scoffs at the "distance run" statistic in today's game, not least because it fails to measure how much energy could have been saved by positioning yourself better and not having to run as much. What's more, Alonso says he has learned, bad things happen when you focus too much on the ball. "You need to be watching what is happening around *you*," Alonso says, "more than what is happening on the ball."

Another benefit of experience for Alonso as he entered his 30s was knowing what he didn't need to do training-wise. Even in his final playing season, Alonso started most of the games for Bayern Munich, which played so frequently that Alonso didn't need to use his practice sessions for physical conditioning. "The body changes," he says. "Now I train more frequently but for less volume. Mostly for me, when I am in season, the training is the game. My trainings are more for recovery and preparation."

English is Alonso's third of four languages, after Spanish and Basque and ahead of German, but he can still speak colloquially, thanks to his five years at Liverpool. One expression he picked up there was *old-school*, which he often deploys to describe his approach to the game and everything around it. What's old-school for Xabi Alonso? His cleats, for one thing. "My boots are like a guitar for a guitar player," he says. "I need to have the right feeling with the ball, with the right studs, and I'm quite a maniac about it. I'm more old-school. I like real leather, so I can have a real fit. I tried synthetic, but it's not for me." Likewise, Alonso says he wore the same shin guards—not just the same type, but literally *the same pair of shin guards*—for the final 13 seasons of his career. Small and light, they fit perfectly and were never broken. He never saw the need to change.

Alonso is so old-school, in fact, that even in the early days of his career he was identifying with some of the most experienced players he was playing against. He says that, at age 19, when he was starting out at Real Sociedad, he marveled at Brazilian World Cup winner Mauro Silva, who was playing his position at Deportivo La Coruña. "He was like a commander on the pitch," says Alonso, who remembers every detail of going up against Silva as a teenager. "Twice I went shoulder to shoulder against him, and I couldn't even move him. He was solid as a rock." When Alonso moved to Liverpool at age 22, he developed an even greater appreciation for the French World Cup winner Patrick Vieira after playing against him during Vieira's last season with Arsenal. "His presence, what a leader he was," says Alonso. "He had so much authority with his teammates, so much respect from the players and the referee." More than a decade later, Alonso was viewed the same way by his peers. And, like Vieira, who had gone on to be the manager of NYCFC, Alonso was set on moving into the coaching ranks.

Much as Pulisic's ability to take on defenders one-on-one is nearly fully formed as a teenager, Alonso's passing talents at 19 were at the level of a veteran's. In Alonso's eyes, completing a pass isn't just about picking a target and sending the ball to your teammate. He takes into account the weight and distance of the pass, the location of defenders, the preferences of the player receiving the ball, and whether Alonso himself was passing to feet or to space, on the ground or in the air.

"When I make a pass, my goal is for [my teammate] to have the best possible way, on the right foot or left foot, to have an advantage," he says. "Of course, [my teammate] has to be in the right position. That's *his* job. But, for example, if I pass to the left, he may have more problems to turn, so I pass to his right foot. That's my idea: to create a pass with an advantage, not to create a problem. That is something that comes with the game, with the space, with the quality of player that you have [receiving it]. I think really quickly because it comes natural to me. I know if I have to play a flat pass or a pass with spin. Each ball and each situation can be different."

Because Alonso touched the ball so often in any given possession, he could influence the tempo of his team's passes, adjusting the metronome to a higher frequency to put pressure on the opposition, or to a lower frequency to settle the game down. Throughout, risk management was always on his mind. When you're closer to the goal in the attacking end, he says, you should take passing risks, because one good pass can turn into a goal. But in your own end a risk would be foolish and could result in the ball finding your own net.

Even when Alonso's side had possession, he was thinking about his teammates' collective shape, should a turnover occur. "When the strikers are attacking," he says, "I have to think: If they lose the ball, where should I be positioned to regain it as quickly as possible? Sometimes, depending on your position, you need to press high. But if you're more exposed, you need to take a step back and try to defend the space, rather than the man. You need to distinguish those moments." That discerning power is part of what Alonso studied so closely under Guardiola. During the game, however, it can't come from a coach. It has to be internal.

In November 2015 Bayern Munich hosted Arsenal for a Champions League group-stage match. Bayern had lost 2–0 in the first leg, two weeks earlier, and Alonso says preparations for this game—mostly through video study—were as intense as ever under Guardiola. The clips the coach showed were focused on Arsenal as a team, Alonso explains, but "you can ask for video of the players around your position. For example, I know [Gunners midfielder] Mesut Özil pretty well [from their time together at Real Madrid], but I didn't know as well how he was playing with his Arsenal teammates. When he was playing to Theo Walcott, he would play more to the space [in front of Walcott]." Similarly, Alonso studied Arsenal's Alexis Sánchez. "Some wingers, they close in to the middle," he says, "and if they close in, there will be space outside. We know that Alexis has more of a striker's mentality, so he will leave open the space between the central midfield and the winger. That's the position we wanted to exploit." Sure enough, Bayern's first two goals come from crosses in which Arsenal—not just Sánchez—fails to put pressure on a passer positioned out wide.

Listening to the vocabulary Alonso uses while watching different video clips from the game against Arsenal is an education in itself: "Here you know that [forward Olivier] Giroud is really good holding the ball. So, more than defending him close, you need to give him a distance because he uses the ball really well. He tries to leave the ball to players, so I will try to protect somehow, him or the space . . . Here is where you are willing to take risks, because a good pass could give a chance to score a goal. So instead of taking the easy way to play back, it's better to create ... Here you try to give him an option to pass to you, to be a solution ... Here you try to defend more of the space, maybe, more than the man ... Arsenal, they are not the most aggressive team, so they leave room to play ... Here again, Arsenal don't press that much ... Here we were winning, so I took the safe pass to keep the ball. In a more risky position, I would look forward, rather than backward. Different games, different tempos ... Özil is not one of those players who stays in the number 10 position. Sometimes he comes to each side. I need to talk to the fullbacks for a plan to control him and to help me, and maybe I will come between the centerbacks."

You get the picture. A few words stand out when Alonso speaks about the game. One is *control*, which is the most common word he uses to describe Bayern's objective when it has possession of the ball. *Control* also comes up in a defensive context in terms of Alonso's task of helping to contain Özil or Sánchez. Another word that Alonso deploys frequently is *desperate*, which he almost spits out in disdain. Desperation results when your positioning has been wrong, and faulty positioning is a cardinal sin in the World According to Xabi. It's why he dislikes slide tackles. During a Bayern possession, I ask Alonso: How often do you make a late run into the box? "Rarely," he replies. "It would be a desperate solution. I would be more worried of holding this position and holding this player, rather than being the man to score the goal."

By halftime it's a 3–0 blowout, and Bayern is dominating possession. Alonso's distribution is impeccable, a kind of Chinese water torture: mostly short passes with the occasional long-distance arrow. Why short passes? So much of the modern game is about transitions, the decisive moments in which possession is lost and the team that has won the ball can advance on a foe that's slightly unbalanced or disorganized. In most cases, Alonso says, he would prefer that his team make two or three short passes rather than one long pass, the better to keep his teammates in a compact shape, ready to defend as a unit should they lose the ball. "When you're playing long passes, your players have much more distance between each other," Alonso explains, "and when they lose the ball, it's harder to get the ball back because they can't pressure as well together."

When Guardiola was coaching Bayern Munich, he would tell his players to connect a minimum of 15 passes before looking to play forward because that would ensure they had time to get their positional structure right and establish control so that if they did lose the ball, the players would be close enough together to press in unison and win it back immediately.

How you attack and how you defend—those are inextricably linked, and no player is more responsible for a team's combined approach than a defensive midfielder like Alonso. Against Arsenal he is in complete control, at the center of everything, like a conductor whose symphony surrounds him on all sides. When Bayern finishes off its 5–1 victory, it's hard to remember a single play that Alonso made. Yet in his own way he was the most dominant player of the game.

In the last three seasons of his playing career, Alonso was almost like a player-manager, even if he didn't have the coaching aspect on his official job description. He was preparing himself for the next phase of his soccer journey. When it comes down to it, though, Alonso is smitten, hopelessly in love with his sport.

It fills his thoughts, his conversations, even his dreams. In an interview that takes place on a Champions League Tuesday, he says he'll be watching on the television that night, even though Bayern has the week off.

How does Alonso watch a game on TV? What does he look for? "I don't just follow the ball," he says. "I follow more the other positions. But the TV cameras are focusing [on the ball], so it isn't very good for the tactical analysis of the game. You need a wider perspective to have a better analysis. But I love watching football. For sure I am watching tonight: to learn from the football side, the tactical side, and the emotional side. You never know what is going to happen and how you have to approach those difficult moments, how a manager decides or how a player behaves. I like to watch these things as well."

If you're Xabi Alonso, your education never ends.

IN PULISIC'S CASE, HIS TEENAGE talent for beating defenders in one-on-one battles is almost a finished product. Claudio Reyna, who's now the sporting director for MLS's NYCFC, says: "What he has that I don't recall too many U.S. players having is real 1v1 technical ability to get by players in a consistent way by unbalancing them at speed. He's not the fastest guy, but he finds a way, which I think is kind of an art in itself, to just get by people. You see it at Dortmund all the time. He's just always skinning players."

Yet for all the things that Pulisic can already do on the field— and we've detailed many of them here—it's worth reminding everyone that he still has a lot to improve on if he wants to take the next steps. "It's not sexy," Reyna says, "but he needs to get better on the defensive side of the game, and that'll come with age and a little more physicality." European soccer is a punishing sport. In a typical calendar year, Pulisic will play around 65 competitive games: perhaps 50 for Dortmund (in the Bundesliga, German Cup, and Champions League) and 15 for the U.S. national team. Those don't include Dortmund's preseason games or games during Germany's winter break in January. All told, players usually have only six weeks off each year from mid-June to the end of July, and not even that happens in a World Cup year. The miles add up. By the time he was done at Manchester United, Wayne Rooney looked like the oldest 31-year-old in the world.

German soccer has slightly fewer *English weeks*, the term Germans use for playing games every three or four days for months, owing to the Bundesliga's smaller number of teams (18) than the 20 in the English Premier League and to Germany having one domestic knockout competition compared to England's two (the FA Cup and the League Cup). But playing 65 real games a year starting at age 17 is a daunting challenge. "Growing and becoming stronger and working in the gym—that's been big for me this season [2016–17]," Pulisic says. "The wear on your body is a lot, and you have to take care of yourself." Learning how to use his strength has been a challenge. The hardest part of his job as an attacking midfielder, he says, is receiving balls in tight areas when there's a big defender right on his back. "It's those times when you know it's not time to be creative right now," he explains. "I have to be strong and use my body and just hold up and keep possession, because that's all you can do in those situations or you're just going to get killed."

If you ask Pulisic which skills he had before he went to Dortmund at age 15 and which ones he has done more to acquire since joining the club, he pauses to flash back in time in his head for a moment. "I think I had a good dribbling ability always, starting even with youth national teams," he says. "In tight spaces, I could kind of maneuver my way out of them and dribble, and I was always creative. A big part of my game this season has been trying to become more clinical—in front of goal, crossing, passing. I know I still have a lot of work to do, and that's what people criticize the most. But one of the toughest parts of soccer is bringing a play to the end and finding the right pass, taking the right shot, or whatever it is."

We hear the word *clinical* so often in soccer discussions that it has become something of a cliché. But for Pulisic the term comes down to *efficiency* in the most important part of the field, the opposing penalty box. The hardest thing to do in soccer is to score a goal, to have the judgment to know what to do in the box to produce results as consistently as possible. What's the point of beating a defender one-on-one to burst into the box if you make the wrong decisions on passing or shooting once you get there?

Learning to be clinical, Pulisic says, "is so many different things. It just comes down to your focus in the end, and how perfect you want to make that pass or shot and just make it easier on your teammates and for yourself when you have to finish in the right times." In his first full season in the Bundesliga, Pulisic studied the task of crossing the ball in the same way a high school senior (which is what he would have been in the United States at the time) might study calculus. Some of it was fairly basic: Once you beat a player, pull your head up to scan the landscape for crossing targets.

But there's a more advanced level to crossing, too, he says.

"Something I'm learning now," Pulisic explains, "is when you look up and you don't have a lot of options there. You can whip in a ball at the proper speed, whether it's a chipped ball to the back post or it's just a driven one across the goal, right in front of the goalkeeper. Those are just very tough to defend. You figure out whether you want it on the ground or if you want it a little higher. If it's higher, like waist-height, it's much harder to defend."

To explain, Pulisic breaks down a play from a Champions League game against Legia Warsaw. Racing down the left side on a five-on-four break, Pulisic receives a pass in the box from Emre Mor. His head up, Pulisic knows he's going to hit a first-time cross with his left foot—this is no occasion for futzing around with multiple touches and losing the advantage—but he doesn't see an obvious target. Three Dortmund teammates are in the box. He could dink a short cut-back pass to Raphaël Guerreiro. Or he could send a cross into the prime space between the goalkeeper and Aubameyang (in the middle) or Gonzalo Castro (racing in from the right). Ultimately, Pulisic decides to aim for the space and not a particular player. His cross shadows the line of the six-yard box waist-high. Aubameyang is defended well and can't reach the ball, but Castro beats his man to the cross for an easy finish. "This is all about just putting it in front of the goalie in a dangerous area," Pulisic says. "I didn't specifically see Castro on this play. But you know you've got runners in the box."

When it comes to clinical shooting, Pulisic explains, one of the best tips he ever received is something simple: Put the ball on target. If your shot has no chance to go in the goal, you can't score. That said, you also have to be precise in your accuracy as a shooter, in much the same way that a baseball pitcher has to paint the corners of home plate for most of his strikes. The size of the goal—eight feet high by eight yards wide—has been the same since it was codified by the English Football Association in 1882. How much taller are goalkeepers today than they were in the 19th century? Well, one recent study revealed that the average height of male army conscripts in the Netherlands—the home of 6-foot-5 goalkeeping great Edwin van der Sar—had grown by 8.3 inches from 1858 to 1997. The height increase of human beings over the last century was what led Major League Soccer to have serious talks about making the goals larger before the league started in 1996.

In the end, MLS kept its goals the same size, due to entreaties from FIFA, but the fact remains that 21st-century goalkeepers make it extremely hard to find open space in the goal for shooters. "It's just finding the corners and sides of the goal, taking what the goalie's giving you," says Pulisic, noting that placement is often more important than power on a shot. "Honestly, I don't even remember a goal of mine yet in professional soccer where it's just been a rip, a power shot, which is kind of interesting to think about. But you look at Messi's two goals yesterday, and I don't know how his little body gets so much power on his shots. It's pretty incredible."

On the previous day, Lionel Messi had been at his imperious best in Barcelona's 3–2 win at Real Madrid, dominating the world's biggest rivalry game and scoring two goals, his second one coming as the match-winner in the 92nd minute to silence the Estadio Bernabéu. Pulisic watched every second. He has had a special connection to the city of Barcelona ever since his first trip there at age 7 with his family and three separate training stints at

FC Barcelona's famed La Masia academy, starting at the age of 10. While watching *El Clásico*—or any other game, for that matter— Pulisic doesn't digest the scene the same way most viewers might.

"You kind of put yourself in their shoes and you think, like, OK, if I'm in that situation, what could I do? You see what he does and then you're thinking like, Was it a good play? What could I have done to really open that play up more or have done a little better? It's just watching them and learning. Learning from some of the greats. Messi showed his magic yesterday, and he's at another level than any player in the world. But I love watching a lot of the Barça players—actually that entire mid- field, including Iniesta and Busquets—and what they do and how simple they play. And I love watching some of the other players around Europe, like [Paris Saint-Germain's] Neymar and [Chelsea's Eden] Hazard, because I do want to kind of model myself after their games."

It's all coming so fast these days. When a gifted teenager makes The Leap, rising from complementary player to star, im- provement can happen in a matter of weeks or months, not years. When Christian Pulisic played in the Copa América Centenario in June 2016, he didn't start any of the U.S.'s six games. By the time he joined the U.S. camp five months later in Columbus, he was the best player on the team. Getting better feeds on itself. If you realize hard work can take you to a new level, chances are you'll keep the habit and not feel satisfied until you reach that level.

Pulisic's production in the Bundesliga has already been re- markable. In modern soccer, a terrific tool for using data to mea- sure goal chances and creation is the expected goals model. Goal scoring is a process driven to a large extent by randomness. A player can get into a great position and take a dangerous shot, only to be denied by an even better save. In this situation, the shooter would not get any credit just from counting goals. Likewise, a player can take a bad shot from a bad location and score from a lucky deflection.

To look past some of this luck and seek more information about each shot taken, we can use expected goals. Each shot's expected goal value (xG) is calculated by comparing it to hundreds of thousands of other shots, based on a range of attributes. These include the location of the shot, whether it was assisted by a cross, whether it was a header or part of a counterattack, and many more considerations. We can then estimate the probability of a shot being scored. This is the expected-goal value—if the shot was taken over and over again, what proportion of the time would you expect a goal to be scored? Naturally, a higher probability of scoring means the chance was of higher quality.

The company Opta has a massive soccer database. Using that database for this book, the analyst Ben Torvaney unearthed some revealing examples of Pulisic's production in 2016–17, his first full season in the Bundesliga. Going into a season at age 17, only two players in Spain's La Liga, the German Bundesliga, and the English Premier League since 2013–14 clocked more minutes on the field than Pulisic's 1,515 minutes for Dortmund in 2016–17. (Those players were Timo Werner and Max Meyer, both also in the Bundesliga.) What's more, according to Opta's expected-goals model, Pulisic had 0.22 expected goals per 90 minutes, an impressive value that was nearly equal to that of then-teammate Ousmane Dembélé (0.23), who was subsequently sold to Barcelona for €105 million ($124.6 million). Even more eye-popping was Pulisic's production when it came to chance creation. As Torvaney notes, we can use the same metric (xG) to get information about the quality of chances a player has created by looking at the xG values of the shots for which they have provided the passes. By this metric, Pulisic created 0.26 xG per 90 minutes for teammates in 2016–17. Going into a La Liga, Bundesliga, or Premier League season aged 20 or younger since 2013–14, only six players have assisted on more expected goals than Pulisic did as an 18-year-old in 2016–17. None of those other players was younger than 19 when he did. And of that same group of top-three league players 20 or younger since 2013–14, only 14 players had produced a season better than Pulisic's 3.3 winning dribbles versus an opposing player every 90 minutes.

Yet if you ask Pulisic to be honest about the aspects of his game that need work, you had better be prepared to listen for a while. "My crossing and finishing ability," he says. "Being consistent and clinical in those situations, and specifically where to put the ball on passes and shots, and how hard to hit it, and the right direction. Growing as a player, becoming stronger, working on my dribbling and decision making in the right times. When to go by a player, or to make a simple pass, or to just pick your head up and find a ball in behind, like I did for Clint and I do for Aubameyang all the time."

Pulisic has the chance to make it (eventually) because he knows he hasn't made it yet.

EVERYONE HAS A CHRISTIAN PULISIC origin story.

Claudio Reyna was U.S. Soccer's youth technical director when he first saw the 12-year-old Pulisic at a U.S. Under-14 national team camp. The youngster was tiny at that age, younger and smaller than the other boys on the field, but Reyna says you could tell even then that the kid was special. "He was a small, quick technical player," Reyna says, "and you could see he just loved playing and had a real energy about him. He wanted to score goals. He was an offensive player who was confident on the ball. He just had this kind of continued progression. The things you saw at a young age, he just got better and better with. They're traits he still has today."

Tab Ramos, like Reyna, is one of the most technically gifted midfielders in U.S. history. Ramos, who's now the U.S. Under-20 coach, was coaching an Under-16 team at a U.S. Soccer Development Academy event in the Washington, D.C., area one time when he happened to walk past a game involving the Under-14 teams of D.C. United and PA Classics, a club based in Lancaster, Pennsylvania. What Ramos saw that day still stands out to him like a lightning bolt. On the field was a remarkably small 11-year-old who was bossing an Under-14 game.

"He looked like someone's little brother who just jumped on the field, and I was waiting for someone to get him out," says Ramos. "Then I realized, 'Wow, not only does he look like he doesn't belong physically, but he's running the show. *This kid is running the show.*' He clearly was younger, smaller, and didn't look like he belonged in the game until he was around the ball. And until you watched the game for about five minutes and you realized that everybody was playing through him. And the pace of the game was completely run by him."

Before he was finished walking around the field, Ramos called U.S. Soccer's director of scouting, Tony Lepore, and told him about Pulisic. Lepore replied that he was "aware" of the young man from Pennsylvania. Looking back, Ramos says you didn't need an extensive scouting network to realize that Pulisic had the ingredients to be the real thing. It was that obvious. "I've coached all the way from Under-10s to U-18s," Ramos says. "I've coached a lot of games, probably about 400 to 500 youth games through 9 or 10 years with multiple teams to get a lot of experience. I've never come across a situation like that. That was the only time. I recall it like it was yesterday, because it's not the norm."

Michael Zorc, the sporting director of Borussia Dortmund, has his own Pulisic origin story. Zorc, whom you'll get to know later in this book, is one of the most respected talent spotters in soccer. He *has* to be because his competition, Bayern Munich, is blessed with enough wealth not just to buy superstars from around Europe but also to poach Dortmund's best players, as Bayern has done repeatedly over the years. "We have a rival who makes €200 million [$217 million] more per year in revenues," Zorc says on a rainy fall day in Germany's Ruhr Valley. "So we have to have a different approach to compete with them. We have to be quicker in finding young talent."

Dortmund casts a global net in its pursuit of prospects. In January 2014, Zorc sent his scouts to a youth tournament in Turkey to take a close look at the U.S. Under-17 national team and its promising forward, Haji Wright. But a funny thing happened that week: While they were observing Wright, Dortmund's scouts fell in love with a slight, 15-year-old midfielder on the same team who possessed a combination of speed, vision, and soccer IQ that Zorc had never seen in an American his age. "We said, 'Hey, [Wright] is a really good player, but there's one fantastic, outstanding player,'" Zorc says of Pulisic. "From this time we followed him and tried to realize the transfer."

Pulisic moved with his father, Mark, to Germany in the summer of 2014, and in 2016 he broke through with Dortmund and the U.S. national team to become the best American male soccer prospect since Landon Donovan in the early 2000s. In April 2016, Pulisic scored his second goal in the German Bundesliga, the youngest player ever to do so (17 years, 218 days). Five months later, he was the most dangerous attacking player in the U.S.'s 4–0 World Cup qualifying win over Trinidad and Tobago, his first national team start. And three weeks after that, Pulisic came on against Real Madrid in a Champions League game and delivered the cross that led to Dortmund's equalizer in a 2–2 tie. "He's the kind of guy who's very confident and doesn't show any nerves under pressure," Thomas Tuchel, Dortmund's manager at the time, told me. "That's a wonderful combination."

The world soon began to notice, too. In the fall of 2016, Pulisic signed a lucrative deal through 2022 with Nike, which has been aching to find the first U.S. men's soccer superstar. In the 2016 summer transfer window, Pulisic was the subject of offers—from Liverpool, RB Leipzig, and other clubs—worth as much as $20 million, which would have made him one of the most expensive 17-year-olds of all time. "There have been some offers for him in the summer window from England and from German clubs," Zorc told me in October 2016, "but we would like to have him here and develop him here. We didn't educate him to sell him."

Of course, Pulisic's soccer education started many years earlier, back when Mark Pulisic started calling his son "Figo" (which he still does). Mark and Kelley Pulisic say they didn't put undue pressure on Christian from an early age; they let him play a variety of sports, not just soccer, and they wanted to make sure it was fun for him. Still, from the time Christian was three, Mark would kick the ball toward his son's left foot so that he could work on his weaker peg. At the time, the Pulisic family would regularly watch Real Madrid's *Galácticos* on television. Christian's favorite player was the former World Player of the Year Luís Figo, not least because of the way the Portuguese star would take on opponents out wide and dribble past them and be courageous with the ball (much as Pulisic plays today). Christian's first jersey was Figo's Real Madrid shirt.

The highest levels of soccer are far easier to watch on U.S. television these days than they were in the 20th century, and, as a result, young Americans can grow up much more easily with soccer in their blood. The United States has always had high participation numbers in the sport, but the ubiquity of pro soccer on television now gives those players something to aspire to and makes *watching* it a regular part of their lives. The culture change of soccer on American television may well help bring more U.S. players to the elite ranks in the years to come. The idea makes sense: If a 13-year-old American soccer player can consume that much soccer on TV, pick up the finer points of the sport, and see that Lionel Messi and Cristiano Ronaldo make millions of dollars, maybe that young American won't quit the sport and choose another one because that's the only way he thinks he can become a professional athlete. Pulisic is just one example of the new generation of American kids who've had the chance to be regular viewers of European soccer—and the benefits were palpable. "As he was playing U-12, U-14, and U-16, you could tell he watched," says Mark of his son's soccer IQ. "He was trying things that he saw. He was tactically aware, and a lot of that came from seeing games."

What's more, Christian revealed a competitive streak early on. Claudio Reyna says that when he has spoken to soccer talent developers, especially in the Netherlands, they have noted that one area in which young American players excel globally is in their all-out push to win. The U.S. culture might not produce as many skilled players, but, man, they hate to lose. That's no small thing. Sam Hinkie, the former NBA general manager, once told *Sports Illustrated*'s Chris Ballard that, in selecting a player, he wished he had access to the sum total of the scores of every game an athlete had played in his life, going back to childhood board games. Pulisic would have scored well on Hinkie's test. As Mark Pulisic says, "Any type of sport we would play outside, whether it was Nerf basketball, H-O-R-S-E, throwing a baseball or an American football, he was just determined to win everything. When he didn't win everything, he wasn't happy."

Early on, Pulisic's parents observed a formidable intensity in Christian. Mark remembers five-year-old Christian teaching himself how to shimmy up a vertical wall at their house "like Spider-Man," he says. "It was the most incredible thing. We used to bring people over to see this, and he was so determined. *I can do this, I can do this.* He would go all the way to the top of the ceiling, and my wife and I would be so scared. Then he would touch the ceiling and shimmy his way back down."

Meanwhile, the pace of Christian's soccer progression was breathtaking. At 7, he absorbed English football culture while living with his family for a year near Oxford while his mother, Kelley, a teacher, was on a Fulbright scholarship. At 8, Christian attended training sessions with his father's indoor team, the Detroit Ignition, and the Brazilian players would challenge the youngster to learn ball tricks (which he would perform the following week). At 10, through his father's coaching contacts, Christian trained for a week at Barcelona's famed La Masia youth academy.

Even though Pulisic grew up adoring Luís Figo when he was playing for Real Madrid, the young American fell in love with the city of Barcelona and its most famous attraction, Barça. Christian first visited Barcelona on vacation with his family at age 7, and he got to see the team play at the Camp Nou stadium. Like so many others, he was blown away by Ronaldinho at the height of his powers. When Christian trained at the Barça academy three years later, his ready adaptation gave a glimpse of what was to come a few years later when he moved to Germany. "The experience was priceless," says Mark, "because he was able to adapt at a young age to being outside his comfort zone. When you're a 10-year-old child and you're going to Barcelona with all the players speaking a foreign language and he's an American kid coming in, it's not an easy thing, you know? All those experiences made him a bit stronger mentally."

Christian performed well enough in his training stint that Barça invited him back for two more in the subsequent years, though Mark says there was never an official trial. "We just enjoyed going to Barcelona, to be honest," the father says. "He impressed them, but he wasn't ready, and they weren't ready to commit to such a young player when so many different things can change." Clearly, though, the Barcelona mystique remains strong with Christian, who watches Barça games with a mix of wonder and appreciation, not just for Messi but also for Iniesta, Busquets, and others. It's hardly a wild fantasy to imagine that Pulisic might someday play for Barça. Not only would Pulisic's skills fit well with Barcelona, but he would also be a good match for the club's desire to become bigger in the United States.

At the same time that he was training as a preteen at Barcelona, Pulisic was playing with the PA Classics youth club, and he joined the U.S. Under-17 residency program in Florida in 2013, when he was 14. Small for his age, he couldn't rely on size to dominate the youth ranks. "I had to use other ways," he says, "and try to outthink opponents even more." The high point of those formative years came in December 2013, when Pulisic's U.S. U-17 team thumped Brazil 4–1 to win the Nike International Friendlies event. Highlights of the game show Pulisic, still undersized at age 15, clowning Brazilian defenders on his way to a goal and an assist, and tournament MVP honors. "That event was the biggest I've had in my career," he says. "It really changed my mind-set on the game. I realized that I can take this game somewhere, that I can do this. That changed everything."

In the immediate aftermath of that game, the stream of agents and other influencers contacting the Pulisics became a flood. Pulisic's father recalls holding a family conference with his wife, his daughter, and Christian about the possibility of Christian and Mark moving to a club in Europe. "We spoke with Christian, and he looked us in the eye and said, 'I'm not ready. I'm not ready to go,'" says Mark. "We said that's no problem."

At the Aegean Cup in Turkey, a month after the Nike International Friendlies, Dortmund saw Pulisic and the club joined other European teams in pursuit. A few months later, the family had another discussion. This time Christian decided he was interested in exploring the possibilities of a move. The family hired the agent Rob Moore, and Christian and Mark made visits all around Europe—to Chelsea, Porto, PSV Eindhoven, Villarreal, and Dortmund—but Dortmund stood out for its history of developing young talent and for its warm welcome of the family by the club's senior figures. "The first day we were here, we met some incredible people," says Mark. They included the sporting director Zorc; Under-17 coach Hannes Wolf, who would eventually take over as the head coach of Stuttgart and lead that club to promotion to the Bundesliga in 2017; and Dortmund's charismatic first-team coach at the time, Jürgen Klopp, who would go on to manage Liverpool. "Here's a 15-year-old kid," marvels Mark, "and Jürgen Klopp comes over and gives me a big hug and gives him a big hug. We're like, 'Wait a minute, this club is huge, and they're really taking their time to make my son feel so welcome.'"

"I kind of knew it was the right place for me," says Christian, "and it's been the best decision." But that doesn't mean the transition in the fall of 2014 was easy. Pulisic was dropped into a German public high school but didn't speak the language. "I only did well in English and art class," he says. Nor did it help to be separated from his friends, his mother, and his siblings, Dee Dee and Chase. "It was a sacrifice, especially in the first six months not knowing the language," says Pulisic, who became fluent with daily lessons and was conducting interviews in German by the fall of 2016. "Every day, even now, I'm still missing home. I don't think people understand that aspect of it. It's not just some crazy, amazing life all the time. You miss home every single day. During the first six months I wasn't able to play in games because I didn't have European citizenship at the time. I was working so hard to try to get a spot on the team, and knowing I couldn't play on the weekend was just heartbreaking."

A controversial FIFA rule prevents players younger than 18 from making international transfers, with a few limited exceptions. The rule is intended to protect minors—many from Africa—from being signed by clubs and discarded onto the streets of a foreign land when they don't make the team. Pulisic's grandfather, though, was born in Croatia, which (in a fortuitous coincidence) had joined the European Union in July 2013, meaning that any of its citizens were free to work anywhere else in the EU. Mate Pulisic had grown up in Croatia before moving to the United States in his early 20s. The Pulisics realized after the Nike Friendlies that Christian had the talent to move to Europe before he turned 18, so they started the process of gaining Croatian citizenship, first for Mark and then for Christian. Although there was a mountain of paperwork, the process ended up moving faster than anticipated. Christian secured a Croatian passport in January 2015, allowing him to play for Dortmund 20 months earlier than he would have without it. "Christian was very fortunate," says Mark. "He was able to start right away with the U-19s and be seen by the first-team coaches and be invited into the training sessions with the pros."

What would Christian have done at Dortmund had he not been able to secure an EU passport so quickly? Mark says there were discussions with Dortmund about the possibility of sending Christian back to the United States to get game experience somewhere. But, fortunately, he says, they never had to worry about that once the passport came through. And even though Christian technically could have played for Croatia instead of the United States, he says there was never any doubt in his mind that he would choose the Stars and Stripes. Once Pulisic played in a World Cup qualifier for the United States against Guatemala on March 29, 2016, in Columbus, Ohio, he was cap-tied to Uncle Sam for good.

Borussia Dortmund is known for its willingness to integrate young players and give them time on the field, and Pulisic's case was no different. Dortmund's motto might as well be: *If you're good enough, you're old enough.* "He started on the Under-17 team when he arrived in Dortmund," said Zorc in October 2016, "and then in time we took him to our professional training. Jürgen Klopp was the head coach at this time, and he could very easily see his outstanding talent. [Pulisic] was able to adapt to another level. There was no difference when he was 17 in training between him and the other professional players already. So last January we took him completely to our [first-team] squad." It shouldn't have been surprising that Klopp's Liverpool had tried to pry Pulisic away from Dortmund with a lucrative transfer offer the previous summer. Klopp knew exactly what the young American brought to the table.

Pulisic continued to show his mettle during his first full season with Dortmund's first team in 2016–17. Dortmund had signed four new attacking players the previous summer, signaling that Pulisic might receive less playing time (and leading to those transfer offers). But, instead, the young American convinced his then-manager, Tuchel, that he deserved to be on the field, and he ended up becoming a regular in Dortmund's rotation, often as a starter. "There's always competition in professional sports, and I knew that," Pulisic says. "Everyone was asking me, What are you going to do with all these new players?

It was just keep training hard every day and earn your position and the respect of the team."

One of the hardest challenges for Freddy Adu as a 14-year-old rookie in 2004, when he was the highest-paid player in MLS, was doing the little things every day—on the field and in the locker room—that would earn the respect of his older teammates. Pulisic's situation at Dortmund was far different from Adu's at D.C. United, of course. Not only was Pulisic older than Adu, but the infrastructure of the club was much more established. Nobody was expecting Pulisic to be the main marketing attraction or the best player. What's more, Pulisic had the help of older teammates who had been in his situation before. In 2005, Nuri Şahin had become the youngest player in Bundesliga history (16 years, 334 days). "On the one hand, you have to get your respect with your football," says Şahin, one of Pulisic's closest friends on the team, "and on the other hand you have to be a good guy in the dressing room. Otherwise, you don't have a chance in your professional life."

It was clear from talking to Şahin that he had developed a genuine affection for Pulisic, not least because Şahin had agreed to an interview with a U.S. reporter *solely about the American*. Şahin had been impressed with Pulisic's skills from the moment he had seen him train for the first time two years earlier. And in their daily interactions the elder German had noted Pulisic's respect for the veterans on the team. "For a young guy, he has already done a lot of things," Şahin said. "He has to decide how far he wants to go. Christian will be a big player if he's down-to-earth, which at the moment he really is. The sky is the limit for him. What is ahead of him could be huge, huge,

huge." Şahin smiled. "I have a Christian Pulisic USA jersey in my locker," he said. "He's wearing the number 10 already!"

While Pulisic's maturity made him sound sometimes like he was about to turn 35, there were still moments when he wanted to be a teenager. In May 2016, while Pulisic was with the U.S. team, then-coach Jurgen Klinsmann agreed to let him go to the high school prom in Pennsylvania the night before a friendly against Bolivia in Kansas City, Kansas. Unable to find commercial flights to get him back in time, Pulisic hired a private jet to take him to the dance and return him to K.C. for the game. "It was one of the best nights of my life," he says. "It was so much fun, and the next day I got to go out and play with my national team and scored my first goal."

By the middle of 2017, though, as he approached his 19th birthday, Pulisic was ready to enter the next phase of his career and be viewed as an adult. The story of his teenage rise to Dortmund's first team had been a whirlwind, and he was proud of it, but he had started a new chapter of his tale now. He no longer needed to live with or be driven to practice by his father. He had his own apartment. He had a full Bundesliga season under his belt and a busy European season to look forward to in 2018. But he still wanted to learn, to get better. If he wanted a role model for how to navigate that path, an ideal one would be Xabi Alonso.

THE WAYS THAT ALONSO AND Pulisic learn about their opponents in advance of a game are similar, though they're always dependent on the decisions of their coaching staffs. Video is the preferred method of communication, and coaches will put together scouting clips detailing the tendencies of both the opposing team as a whole and the individual matchups for Alonso and Pulisic. Starting two days before a game, the entire teams will gather and listen to the manager describe his overall game plan, and then Alonso and Pulisic will spend time on their own looking at video packages of their upcoming foe, tailored to their personal objectives.

"We are playing Saturday against Hamburg," said Alonso during an interview in February 2017. "So Thursday and Friday you try to analyze more specifically how they are going to play. How are they going to think offensively? Defensively? They play 4-2-3-1, so what is their number 10 going to do? Is he going to stay with me? Is he going to press the centerbacks? It changes everything. If he stays with me, I need to change my role. If he leaves my position and goes to press the centerbacks, I need to take another position. We have so much technology to analyze things, and it's important to have an idea of what you're going to face. Then you need to perform that idea on the pitch."

For each game at Dortmund, Pulisic says, the team attends at least two group video sessions in which the coaching staff discusses the opponent's style and the particular strategy BVB wants to deploy in that game. Pulisic says he studies the video clips of his individual matchups, but in general he's more concerned with what he's doing in his attacking midfield position than with how his defender might be countering that. "You can look at one or two things to keep in your mind," Pulisic says, "but if you overthink it and you're looking at everything—all of his plays and what he's doing all the time—then I think you can really only psych yourself out in my opinion. You have to use your strengths, and he should be worrying about you and what you're going to do, and not you about him. You stick to what you're good at. Of course, if there's a foot that you need to force him to or there's a weakness of his, then maybe you can exploit it. I understand that, and I've done it before."

Both Pulisic and Alonso like to watch video of their performances in the game they have just played. Even if you have a photographic memory, Pulisic says, it helps to go back and look at specific plays—on offense and defense—to see if you should have made a different decision. But one area in which Pulisic and Alonso differ is in their use of data to analyze performance. Alonso doesn't see much value in it for his position of defensive midfielder. "For me, my perception or feelings after the game are much more important," he says. "This isn't like baseball or basketball, where you need data. Once the game is over, I have a very clear idea of how involved I have been in the game." When Alonso says he's "old-school," he means it.

The stat-heads get a full workout over at Borussia Dortmund, however. Under Tuchel, Pulisic says, pregame scouting sessions encompassed the data-driven study of an opponent's tendencies, including the side of the field from which a team scores most of its goals. At halftime and after games, Pulisic and his teammates would see their passing percentage, tackles-won percentage, and other updated information on the whiteboard in the locker room. After every game, Pulisic looks at statistics the coaching staff has kept for his top speed, his number of sprints (with and without the ball), his passing percentage, his positional heat map, and his individual tackles-won percentage. "You want to win your own battles and win as many balls against your opponent as you can," Pulisic says. "We look at a lot of numbers after every game. Then in the locker room the next day before training, [the coach] has statistics written on the board to see what we can improve on."

The Dortmund coaching staff also makes sure players are prepared before games on what their exact roles should be during set plays. In modern, data-driven soccer, dead-ball situations are viewed as one area of the sport where more can be done to choreograph routes and take advantage of the opposition. On corner kicks, for example, the 5-foot-8 Pulisic was typically stationed at the top of the penalty box during the 2016–17 season. That often allowed him to shoot from distance when the defense cleared a corner out toward his position. But Pulisic prefers the rare occasions when he's asked to be in the box on corners. As we watch video of the Champions League Round of 16 second leg against Benfica, Pulisic smiles when, stationed at the near post, he flicks a corner kick header to Aubameyang at the far post. Auba heads it home for the equalizing goal, and Pulisic wins some vindication for his heading ability. "At the U-17 and U-19 levels, I actually scored on a lot of headers," he says, "and it was something I always worked on. That was one of the only times they've put me in the box this whole season. Maybe they don't know as much about me, but I do feel strong in the air."

When Dortmund works on possession drills in practice, Pulisic says, the coaches make sure to put players in a position they'll be in during a game. There is no wasted time. Everything the team does to prepare has a purpose, including in-season weight training. Pulisic credits lifting with helping him to grow stronger in the rough-and-tumble Bundesliga, which lasts from August to May. "You don't want to do too much," Pulisic says, "especially right before a game." But he does find it valuable to lift lighter weights with higher repetitions to help increase his strength and stamina for the long haul.

For all the preparation Pulisic goes through, he says he only started thinking about what other teams are doing *to get ready for him* in March 2017. In the wake of his breakout performance in a U.S. jersey—one goal and two assists in a 6–0 World Cup qualifying win against Honduras—his opponents from Panama deployed a clear strategy to manhandle Pulisic in Panama City four days later. Kicking, shoving, tripping—it was all there, and the CONCACAF referee didn't protect Pulisic by issuing the flurry of yellow cards it deserved. A month later, Pulisic is still angry. "Honestly, I never even thought of [being targeted by teams] until the Panama game, when I started getting fouled and kicked the whole first half," he says. "I was thinking to my-self, 'What are these guys watching to think that?' I've never played in a game like that. It didn't feel like a soccer match. [The referee] didn't protect me or the team at all. I was really disap-pointed in that."

When a teenager is already closer than anyone before him to becoming the first U.S. men's soccer superstar, there will be plenty of questions over how he developed on American soil. Is it repeatable? (Why not?) And who developed Christian Pulisic? "He developed on his own," says his father. "He worked hard as a player. I'm not going to take credit. I coached him for many years in his youth. I hope I was a positive influence on his de-velopment, but there were many people involved with that. You can't really pinpoint one or two. My wife and I supported him and made it fun for him. Unfortunately, a lot of parents in the United States don't make it fun for their kids anymore. As I was coaching him, I never wanted to put too much pressure on Christian. We never watched video together. We never made the game into 'work' at such a young age. We always made it fun. So who developed him? My wife and I had a big influence, and he had many great coaches growing up who really believed in allowing Christian to express himself." Ultimately, a variety of factors helped shape Pulisic, including a genetic aptitude and learning basic technical skills with the ball at home between the ages of five and nine.

He may be just a teenager, but Christian Pulisic's relentless pursuit of progress is the definition of the position he plays. "I think I have a very specific style about my game as a creative attacking midfielder," he says one day in his Dortmund apartment. "At the end of every game I ask myself two things: 'Were you confident? And did you change the game in any way?' If you can say you did at the end of the game, then I'm happy with my performance and I can go to sleep at night. And if not, you can see I'm so frustrated about some plays. It bothers me."

But here's the great thing about Pulisic: He'll keep taking on that frustration, one-on-one, until he blows right by it.

2

THE FORWARD

Chicharito Hernández's Scent of Intuition
and the Pursuit of Ugly Goals

THE MOST POPULAR SOCCER TEAM IN THE UNITED STATES IS
the Mexican men's national team. *El Tricolor*, or *El Tri*, as it's
known, regularly fills NFL stadiums, even for meaningless
friendlies. TV ratings for Mexican soccer on U.S. Spanish-
language channels are huge. The Mexican league, Liga MX,
draws bigger audiences on U.S. television than any other soccer league in any language—more than the English Premier
League, more than the UEFA Champions League, and certainly
more than Major League Soccer. When Telemundo won the U.S.
Spanish-language World Cup television rights for the eight-year
period from 2015 to 2022, it paid FIFA $600 million, a full $175
million more than Fox Sports paid for the U.S. English-language
TV rights. Thanks to *El Tri*, no country in the world pays FIFA
more money for World Cup TV rights than the United States.

Mexican *fútbol* is big business in the States, owing to decades-long immigration patterns and the tendency of Mexican-Americans to identify with Mexican soccer as part of their cultural heritage. In fact, Mexico plays more games in the United States than it does in Mexico, not least because its fans in the States have more disposable income than those south of the border.

And so I find myself in a Denver hotel for a rare hour-long audience with two men: Mexican forward Javier "Chicharito" Hernández, his national team's all-time leading goal scorer, and *El Tri*'s manager, the Colombian Juan Carlos Osorio. Why Denver? Well, Osorio has decided to bring Mexico here for altitude training between friendlies in the Los Angeles and New York City areas. And why is this joint interview rare? For starters, national teams don't get together very often; the club game takes up most of the annual calendar. Beyond that, Hernández and Osorio are almost never available for interviews at the same time, and neither one particularly wants to spend time with most of the Mexican soccer media. "They talk about other things," says Osorio, "like Javier's romantic life, blah, blah, blah, blah, blah."

"Everything but football," Hernández says with a laugh, shaking his head.

With his round face, deep-set eyes, and a Roman haircut that he sometimes leavens with gel, Chicharito ("Little Pea" in Spanish) is the personification of the term *Mexican matinee idol*. It would not be folly to presume that as a goal scorer who has played in the satellite television era for Manchester United and Real Madrid—the two most popular soccer clubs on the planet—

Chicharito is known by more people on Earth than any other Mexican in recorded history.

Osorio has one thing he wants to talk about today. "*This* is football," the manager says, pointing with both hands to the elaborate setup he has constructed between us. "*This* is the game." We're seated just outside Mexico's hotel dining room around a knee-high wooden table, on which Osorio has laid out 22 circular tabs—11 green, 11 red—that he carries in a Ziploc bag wherever he goes. Downstairs, fans in green Mexico jerseys are gathered outside the hotel entrance, waiting for the chance to nab autographs from their heroes. In the lobby, a few media members wait for a short group press event taking place later. But upstairs, away from the television cameras, class is in session with *Profe* Osorio. (In Latin countries, coaches are often called *Profe*, short for *Profesor*.) "This is my own crazy idea of preparing my team to play in the last 25 meters," says Osorio, who has been a coach on club teams in Colombia, Mexico, Brazil, England, and the United States. "We need constant movement from our strikers. We try to create patterns. We're taking movement to a new level, and we call it synchronization. The key words are *doubt, movement,* and *synchronization.*"

"Synchronization!" says Hernández, chewing over the English word with satisfaction. "Exactly."

"In the national team, we play with a front three and only one main striker," Chicharito says. "The movements are different" than in the two-forward formations he has often been deployed in at club level with Manchester United, Germany's Bayer Leverkusen, and, more recently, West Ham United.

Movement is Hernández's calling card, and his excitement

while talking about Osorio's innovations is palpable. Some people in this world, many of them elite athletes, are possessed of a laser focus, a preternatural ability to remain calm under any circumstance. Chicharito, by his own admission, is not one of them. When the topic is soccer, he's as animated as a Pixar film. Leaning out of his seat, crouched low and looking you straight in the eye, he jump-cuts from thought to thought as it enters and leaves his racing mind. "I like to breathe, eat, and talk about football," he says during one of our interviews. If you ask him a question about soccer, he might speak for eight minutes straight. Completing a discussion without him leaping atop his seat, like Tom Cruise on *Oprah*, feels like a minor victory.

Chicharito's nonstop movement is precisely what serves him best on the field. Marking him is like trying to defend a puff of smoke in a gust of wind. "I'm a person who cannot be doing nothing," he tells me one day. "I have a deficit. In Mexico we say *hiperactivo*—hyperactive. I am hyperactive! I cannot be standing here like this in my life. I need to keep walking with my phone, speaking. I can't be calm. On the pitch you can probably see that. I'm always *moving-moving-moving*. And I'm a cheeky player. I try to be there and there and there. And if you're standing up, I'll make it look like I'm moving this way and then I move *that* way."

Vincent Kompany knows that well. Kompany, the world-class centerback and captain for Manchester City, has played against Hernández numerous times over the years. Kompany can summon his analysis of Chicharito instantly from deep inside his mental hard drive. "It's not his game to be an all-around forward like Luis Suárez is, perhaps, but in the box I don't think there's a lot of difference between him and some of the best strikers that have ever been playing football, just because he's so lively," says Kompany. "Trying to mark him in the box is nearly impossible because he goes short, he drops back, he goes again, he drops back again. He does about four movements, whereas many strikers just do one powerful movement and try to get there. He'll adapt to wherever you stand to be making use of that, to go into the gap that you've created. Usually for a defender it's more comfortable defending deep and with more bodies. But when you play against Chicharito, you're better off being quite far away from your goal because in the box he's extremely aware of where he's going to have to be to score a goal."

Osorio listens as Kompany's insight is relayed to him, and then he nods. "I agree with him," the manager says. "He will stop and go, and stop and go, and stop and change direction. It's an ability of Javier because he's usually shorter than most centerbacks. That causes them a lot of trouble. I would say that's one of his greatest assets."

Movement is an essential part of the forward's craft. Hernández will never have the open-field explosiveness of Cristiano Ronaldo in his prime, or the cannon shot of Lukas Podolski, or the blinding speed of Thierry Henry, or the height of Peter Crouch, or the sheer trick-filled audacity of Ronaldinho. But Chicharito knows how to move in the penalty box as well as anyone in the sport, and he has worked at making himself proficient in enough other areas as a striker that he has become his own kind of force.

Listen to Xabi Alonso, Hernández's former teammate at Real Madrid: "He is a proper and total striker, like an old-school striker, like Raúl [the former legendary forward for Real Madrid and Spain]. Whenever they say, 'Ah, loose ball in the box,' he is there. He puts the ball in the back of the net. Maybe he is not the quickest, maybe not the most technical, but he is always there. You never know why, but he is always on the scoreline. Those players, maybe they are not the best in any part, but they are so efficient. At United he scored goals. At Real Madrid in just one year he scored goals. At Bayer he's scoring goals. He's a top scorer."

The greatest forward of all time, Pelé, could do everything required to score goals in volume at the highest level. He could beat defenders on the dribble, shoot with speed and accuracy, put himself in perfect position, and rise up to deliver a powerful header. Nobody would say that Chicharito has Pelé's jaw-dropping athleticism, but he does possess the modern forward's requirement that he be capable of doing a range of different tasks to score goals. An apt comparison, in addition to Raúl, would be to the great Dutch goal finder Ruud van Nistelrooy, who also played for Manchester United and Real Madrid.

Chicharito's efficiency and consistency at club level have carried over to his national team. In May 2017, at just 28 years old, he scored his 47th international goal to break Mexico's all-time record, held by Jared Borgetti. A few days later, Hernández sits next to me in Denver with Osorio, who hopes to unleash Hernández even more as a goal-scoring force with his new system of player patterns and synchronization in the Mexican attack. Osorio wants one thing to be clear, however: He and Chicharito are going to show me Mexico's secrets, but they can't come out publicly until this book is released in May 2018.

"Are you sure?" Osorio asks. "May, yes. Not now. You promise?"

"I promise."

"So you will not talk to *anybody* about this?"

"I will not only not print it now for *Sports Illustrated*. I won't even speak about it to anyone privately."

"OK," Osorio says. "So we will show you today."

Chicharito smiles and rubs his hands together. He loves this stuff.

ENGLISH IS NOT HERNÁNDEZ'S FIRST LANGUAGE, and yet his command of it—largely from his four years at Manchester United—is such that he enjoys transporting evocative expressions from Spanish into his newer tongue. Flashing a language maven's smile that brightens a rainy day in 2016 in the German Rhineland, North America's greatest modern striker explains his knack for being in the right place at the right time in the penalty box. "If you're inside the box and a cross is coming," he says, his hair freshly gelled after training at Leverkusen's BayArena, "sometimes you need, as we say in Spanish, to *smell the intuition*, to smell where the cross is going."

Chicharito, who turns 30 in May 2018, grew up absorbing the culture of the game from his father, Javier, and grandfather Tomás Balcázar, both of whom also represented Mexico in a World Cup. He has played in the Champions League for Man United, Real Madrid, and Leverkusen. He is constantly tinkering on the practice field, constantly studying his opponents, his teammates, himself. Like a master sommelier drawing on years of learning to sniff a glass of wine and identify it—South Australia, Clare Valley, 2009 Riesling—the 5-foot-8, 156-pound

Chicharito uses the sum of his experiences to smell an impending cross and decide in an instant which run to make.

What does intuition smell like? "Press play," he says. On the video screen in front of him, he's running down the left side of a four-on-four break, left to right, against archrival Cologne. Leverkusen midfielder Kevin Kampl is advancing with the ball down the right channel and passes it even wider right toward an onrushing Admir Mehmedi. Entering the box at speed in the left channel, Hernández looks to his right, sees all seven players involved—three of his own, four of Cologne's—and processes what he likes to call "the panoramic." Teammate Karim Bellarabi makes a near-post run, pulling centerback Dominic Maroh with him and opening space in front of the goal. Chicharito knows a cross is coming—there's no pressure on Mehmedi out wide—and now he has to decide: Should I continue my run to the far post? Or turn and cut hard to the open space in the middle?

Either way, he will have to beat his marker, right back Marcel Risse. "You play this sport in the mind, not only on the field," Chicharito says. "If [your opponent] is more clever than you, you can be faster and stronger, but probably you are not going to beat him. He's one step in front of you in the mind. On crosses, sometimes I make my move one or two seconds before the ball is coming because I'm trying to guess that the ball is coming there. It's intuition. So I run. Sometimes the ball comes . . . sometimes not. But that intuition is working."

Chicharito cuts hard to his right in the box—into the open space in front of the goal—even before Mehmedi hits a cross, first time toward that expanse. Here, Risse proves an easy mark, ball watching. You half-expect the crouching-tiger Mexican to reach around and tap Risse's far shoulder while racing behind his back like a schoolboy doing a classroom prank. But that one-second jump gives Chicharito the advantage he needs. "If I'm waiting a second more, it's too late," he says, "and the defender will win it." The rest is execution. Hernández's snap-down header bounces off the turf and past goalkeeper Timo Horn into the net.

Intuition. Anticipation. The scent of a goal scorer. Everything about Chicharito's craftsmanship is cool, save for perhaps the mariachi music that blares on the German PA after each one of his strikes.

All four Leverkusen players involved in the break contributed, notes Chicharito, whose goals all have a story in the details. On this one, his early recognition and decisive change of direction doomed Risse, who committed the cardinal sin of what Hernández calls "standing up"—losing focus, remaining flat-footed. "Do you see how I run?" Chicharito asks, rewinding and watching the play in slow motion. "Just two or three steps, and then I beat him because he is standing up. He has no idea. Too late. Football can be so difficult, and that's why making it simple is the hardest thing in this sport. Sometimes you complicate yourself. Sometimes you just need to make one simple pass or run."

Using Opta's statistical database, the analyst Ben Torvaney sought to measure Chicharito's ability to move, anticipate, and sniff out goal-scoring opportunities and create high-quality chances. From open play in the Premier League from the 2010–11 to the 2016–17 seasons, Hernández had the second-highest average expected goals per shot (0.18) of any player with more than 100 shots.

PLAYER	TOTAL SHOTS	xG/SHOT
Mame Biram Diouf (Stoke City)	141	0.18
Javier Hernández (Man United)	123	0.18
Darren Bent (Aston Villa)	165	0.17
Emmanuel Adebayor (Man City, Spurs, Crystal Palace)	183	0.17
Jamie Vardy (Leicester City)	216	0.17
Papiss Demba Cissé (Newcastle United)	156	0.16
Dimitar Berbatov (Man United, Fulham)	149	0.16
Diego Costa (Chelsea)	255	0.15
Danny Graham (Swansea City, Sunderland)	101	0.15
Odion Ighalo (Watford)	146	0.14

SOURCE: OPTA

As Torvaney notes, while no statistics can fully capture the subtleties of a player's actions, that's good evidence of Chicharito's ability to get into high-quality scoring positions. But beyond the quality of each chance, Hernández's ability to put himself in dangerous positions on a regular basis allows him to contribute to the total goal-scoring potential of his team. Of those players with more than 100 shots, Chicharito scored the eighth-most goals per 90 minutes and had the sixth-most expected goals. Hernández's ability to be in the right place at the right time—and find shooting opportunities where others might not—has allowed him to find a place among the Premier League's best strikers.

Here are the top 10 players in expected goals (xG) per 90 minutes over the same seven Premier League seasons.

PLAYER	GOALS	xG	xG/SHOT	SHOTS
Sergio Agüero (Man City)	0.74	0.61	0.13	4.9
Edin Džeko (Man City)	0.62	0.59	0.13	4.6
Robin van Persie (Arsenal, Man United)	0.64	0.57	0.14	4.2
Mario Balotelli (Man City)	0.40	0.55	0.11	5.0
Luis Suárez (Liverpool)	0.63	0.53	0.11	4.9
Javier Hernández (Man United)	0.60	0.52	0.18	2.9
Daniel Sturridge (Chelsea, Liverpool)	0.61	0.50	0.12	4.3
Papiss Demba Cissé (Newcastle United)	0.52	0.49	0.16	3.0
Dimitar Berbatov (Man United, Fulham)	0.57	0.49	0.16	3.1
Harry Kane (Spurs)	0.66	0.48	0.12	4.1

SOURCE: OPTA

Admittedly, Hernández says, it's easier to be part of the ebb and flow of a game when you're in the starting lineup. For much of his time at Manchester United and Real Madrid, Chicharito was used as a supersub, a forward who could come into a game and make a quick difference in the outcome. His manager at United, Sir Alex Ferguson, placed huge value on players who could deliver in such situations. (Ferguson, a lifelong fan of the actor John Wayne, once told me he thought the Duke was the kind of man you could bring on at the end of a game when you needed a goal—a notion that I had not entertained before that.)

Over time, Hernández was so effective in the substitute's role that he became pigeonholed at club level as a reserve—a role that no player desires. Only by moving to Leverkusen did he become a regular starter again. "I was struggling with the rhythm when I came onto the pitch [as a sub]," he says. "I played two or three games and then I'd come back to the bench. When I'm playing more, it's easier in a way to have better results because you are used to the timing of the games. If you're outside watching the game, you don't know the rhythm inside the pitch. So you need to have some time to get used to the rhythm. If you start a game with the 22 players [on both teams], you're in the same rhythm."

Yet there are times when Chicharito is in razor-sharp form, his mobility creating chance after chance, and the goals just don't come. On other occasions, even the chances run dry. Scoring remains the most difficult thing to do in soccer and it keeps getting more challenging. Why?

For starters, the sport is more defensive-minded than it used to be, the result of a century-long evolution in tactics. If you watch a match from any World Cup from the 1960s to the 1980s, for example, it's like viewing a different game. There are more attacking players on the field; the play is more open, with fewer crunching tackles. When a friend sent me the full videos of the World Cup finals from 1966 and 1970, I was dumbfounded by the lack of defensive pressure and its liberating effects on free-wheeling attacks, like Brazil's Pelé-led greats from 1970. These days defenders are deployed in greater numbers, but they're also more physically robust, often ruthless, using extralegal means to short-circuit a dangerous forward. "Defenders kick you without the ball," Hernández says. "They try to get you out of your focus and concentration, either physically or with verbal stuff."

The solution to dealing with an overly rough defender is simple in theory, Chicharito explains: more movement. "Make him run," Hernández says. "When it gets too physical, I like it. It's like a signal. He has doubt. He's taking the game there because he knows if he tries to [defend straight-up] he's going to lose. Even if I'm tired, I'm going to make him run. I want to get more fouls, and it's going to make him even less focused [on the game]." What's more, Chicharito says, he has no problem calling out physical play to the referee. ("My teammates will tell you I'm not a quiet person," he says with a smile.) What bothers him, though, is his perception of a double standard from referees toward fouls committed by a defender on a forward (high threshold for a whistle) and those committed by a forward on a defender (low threshold). If a defender is trying to protect the ball in his own end and gets a love-tap from a forward, Hernández says, there's a 90 percent chance the referee will call a foul. But what are the chances if the tables are turned and the defender does the same love-tap on a forward with the ball? "50-50," he says. "Or even less."

The tangible barriers to goal scoring are severe enough, but they're compounded by the whims of the soccer gods. "You have periods when, even if you close your eyes, you can score a goal," Hernández says. "And then other periods when, even if the goal is open, you put the ball off the crossbar. Why? I don't know. It's a mystery." The key when he misses a scoring chance, he says, is to follow the Bora Milutinović maxim: *What's the most important play? The next one.* "We are human beings," says Hernández. "When you miss a clear chance, obviously that hits you. What I want is to get focused on the *next* one. The one that I missed, I cannot do anything [about that]. The next one is the one I can change."

That equanimity cuts both ways if you're an elite striker. The best forwards have the wisdom and experience to handle not just failure but also success. Finding the elusive balance over a long time frame is one of the keys to sustaining a career in European soccer, Hernández argues. "When you score a hat trick, you want to celebrate," he says, "but you need to be calm. Because the important thing is not the hat trick. The important thing is the next game. They say in my country: 'The easiest thing is to get there, but the hardest thing is to keep it.' So I want to keep it. When I go out and play bad, I need to keep my confidence up. And when I play very good, I need to keep my confidence *lower*. I need to stay always balanced. It's difficult to manage that. I'm not going to feel like the best player in the world if I score a hat trick, and I'm not going to feel like the worst striker if I don't score a goal."

Besides, he says, a forward can play a terrible game and still score, just the same as he can be consistently influential for 90 minutes—setting up his teammates, dragging defenders out of space, moving constantly, pressing high in defense—without hitting the back of the net. "That's football," Hernández says with a knowing shrug. It's one of his catchall phrases to explain the inexplicable that the sport so often presents, especially for forwards. Consider taking penalty kicks, for example. Whenever Hernández is standing over a spot kick, he always decides beforehand which side of the goal he'll aim for. The one exception? When he converted a penalty at the 2013 Confederations Cup against Italy's Gianluigi Buffon, one of the greatest goalkeepers of all time. "I decided to shoot it to my left," Chicharito recalls, "but then I ran and shot it the other way because I looked at him first. Only on that one." *That's football*. The way he sees it, you can practice 100 penalties in training and be successful on all of them. "But then you go shoot one in a game and it's different," he says. "You have pressure, you have another goalkeeper, and you can miss it. That's football. It's not predictable."

What's the most frustrating thing about Chicharito's job? Failing to convert chances is tough, he argues, but even worse is not having any scoring opportunities at all. "If I have six chances and I miss [all] six, of course I'm not going to be happy—but I'm calm because I had the chances," he says. "When you don't even have chances, *that's* the difficult thing."

Chicharito cues up another scene. The opponent, Hannover, is playing a high back line (its deepest defenders closer to midfield), a staple of the modern game for teams that want to keep possession in the attacking end of the field. But soccer is a game of space. If the field is a king-sized bed, a team can only be a queen-sized blanket. Move the blanket up, and it creates a void in the back. Hernández can exploit those high lines with his movement, especially during the early, unbalanced moments of a counterattack.

"I love to run into the channel [the space between an opposing fullback and his closest centerback] and get coordinated with my teammates," he says. "Some forwards are tall and big; we say those are more objective players"—target forwards—"because you can play longballs to them and they can hold the ball [while others catch up and join the attack]. I am not the tallest, not the strongest, not the quickest. But I am quick enough. I am strong enough. And I prefer to move more than be static. I prefer to run into space and receive balls at my feet."

On the screen Kevin Kampl is advancing the ball, right to left, just past midfield in the first stages of a counter. Hannover's high back line has 40 yards of open space behind it, and Chicharito is walking a tightrope: He starts his run into the left channel, making eye contact with Kampl and trusting that his teammate will release a pass while Hernández is still *just* onside with the line of two retreating centerbacks. Kampl nails the timing, rifling a diagonal pass that Chicharito meets 25 yards from the goal. Now the striker is one-on-one with the centerback Marcelo (not to be confused with the Real Madrid fullback of the same name).

If Hernández was entirely reliant on his naturally stronger right foot, Marcelo could cheat toward one direction in marking him. But Hernández is dangerous with either foot—another hallmark of the modern forward. Using Opta data, the analyst Ben Torvaney took the top 10 Premier League players in expected goals per 90 minutes from 2010–11 to 2016–17 (see above) and found the proportion of those expected goals taken by shots with a player's dominant foot. Of those 10 players, only Edin Džeko (46 percent) took a lower proportion with his dominant foot than Chicharito's 50 percent. Being in the right position to strike a loose ball is one thing, but it's quite another to have the ability to make the shot regardless of whether it comes to your left foot, your right foot, or your head.

Back on the field in Germany, Chicharito dips into his bag of tricks. To many people, a "bicycle" in soccer is a dramatic overhead scissor kick. But Spanish speakers call that move a *chilena*, and Chicharito has a different one that he calls the "bicycle." At speed, he steps over the ball with his right foot and slows down just barely, causing Marcelo to lean to his left for a split second. Then Chicharito explodes to his (supposedly weaker) left, blowing past the hapless defender. "Now I'm looking at the ball," Hernández says, "but I can see in the panoramic that the keeper is coming."

Here the forward is raising his wineglass to his nose once again. Shooting on goal is the ineffable skill of a striker, the ability to read the target and balance precision and power to beat the goalkeeper and give yourself the greatest chance of putting the ball in the net every single time. There are no style points for goals. It is a binary proposition. In or out. Yes or no. Success or failure. The only rule is that whatever you do needs to work. In these situations, Hernández has learned to trust his experience and his instincts, for which the most storied clubs in the world have been willing to pay him millions of euros and pounds and pesos. Most professional goalkeepers will protect their near post—it's a cardinal rule of the position—but Chicharito will always check to see if that is the case. If the near post is covered, the far post should have an opening. Shooting lower usually provides more margin for error than aiming for the top corner, but you need to be able to do both. If Hernández is unpressured farther from the goal—say, outside the penalty box—he'll check to see if the goalkeeper is off his line and be prepared to shoot from distance. There are a million little variables, depending on the situation. That's why Chicharito spends so much time in practice working on his shooting, over and over again. "Like golf, you need to kick 300 balls to try and perfect something," he says. "We do that, but sometimes in a game you just need to try something. For example, maybe you think to chip the ball over the goalkeeper. And sometimes you score, and sometimes you look ridiculous."

This particular shot will not require such feats of courage. If the goalkeeper, Ron-Robert Zieler, stays on his line, Chicharito says, "I will try a harder shot across him. But he's coming out. He can't come out standing, so he needs to guess. So I just try to pop it up and put it on his left side." Chicharito jabs a perfectly placed, left-footed dagger—it's more like a pass than a shot—to the keeper's left and into the far right corner of the net.

In a sport where goals are as precious as pearls, the ensuing sensations can verge on the metaphysical. "Go and ask a goalkeeper like Manuel Neuer or Tim Howard: Do you want to score a goal?" Hernández says. "They're going to say yes. *Everyone* who plays this sport wants to score a goal. It's not only strikers. You can see when defenders come up for a corner kick, they *want* to score a goal, because of course it's unbelievable. When you see the ball going into the net"—he snaps his fingers—"I don't think of anything at first. Then I celebrate and say thank you to God, and I dedicate my goals. But when the ball goes into the net, sometimes I don't remember that. You cannot explain exactly those moments. You need to *live* them."

Yet you might be surprised to learn that scoring goals is not Hernández's favorite moment on the soccer field. Scoring is his job, of course, but if you put too much stock in individual feats, he believes, you'll lose sight of the fact that soccer is a team game. No, Chicharito says his favorite moment is the ritual before every game: staying with his teammates at the hotel the night before; walking on the field an hour before the game; visualizing the action in a quiet locker room; and, if it's an international game, marching out and standing together for the national anthems. "Everything that is involved in our game—I love it," he says, "ever since I was a kid and going to the stadium to watch my dad. The environment of football, the first whistle, the emotion, the adrenaline. That's what I love most."

What is a modern forward? For Chicharito, the best ones have to be complete players on and off the field. "I prefer to have a little of everything," he says. "I can move with the ball and without it. I can jump. I can protect the ball. I can finish with my left and with my right. I can cross a ball. I can give an assist to another player. I can defend. And there are always things I want to improve. In the best leagues in the world you play three or four tournaments per year. So training, recovery, staying healthy—that's even more important now. Europe isn't like Mexico or MLS. Here, you don't stop." Even within Europe there are significant differences between nations. Chicharito says England is more physical, while the style in Spain provides more time to think on the ball—a bit more like the way the game is played in Mexico. Germany is a hybrid of Spain and England, he says. "The rhythm can be quicker or slower," he explains, "but you need to put your qualities out there if you're playing in any part of the world." Adaptation is essential, but you only want to change so much of your game.

Using data and video analysis, opposing coaches can isolate more than ever the strengths and weaknesses of a particular player. As part of his evolution in European club soccer, Hernández has worked at his craft, finding new ways to create space for himself in the attacking third of the field. Like a dominant post player in basketball, Chicharito has developed countermoves that apply his skill with both feet. In recent years he has been perfecting another wrinkle. "I'm trying to improve on scoring goals from outside the box," he says. "If they try to stop me [in the box], I need a Plan B."

This time the foe is Borussia Mönchengladbach. Attacking right to left on the screen, teammate Stefan Kiessling is being defended closely on the ball at the top-left corner of the penalty box. Kiessling sees Chicharito facing him, unmarked, eight yards away, just outside the top of the box, and lays off a short pass. Even before Hernández spins to his left, he has processed the scene. ("Panoramic!" he says with a smile.) He has options: (1) Pass the ball into the box; (2) dribble there himself and take on defenders; or (3) shoot from distance. Onscreen, Chicharito's back is to the goal; offscreen, he's like the former basketball star Bill Bradley describing what it's like to have "a sense of where you are" in John McPhee's book of that name. "I don't see the goal, but I *sense* it. I know the goal is there," he says. "When I was a kid, they taught me: You don't need to look at the goal sometimes; the goal is not going to move. But *you* are going to move, so you need to read where *you* are."

With the same decisiveness that he used to score with his left foot against Hannover, Chicharito now completes a spin move and powers a right-footed blast from outside the box. His defender, Håvard Nordtveit, is a split-second late in jumping out at him—and even that action helps Hernández. "He blocked the vision of the keeper," he notes, watching as the shot sails past

Yann Sommer into the right side of the net, one of three Chicharito goals in a 5–0 victory.

There may be mysteries to scoring goals, but there are no mysteries when it comes to improving as a player. It's why Chicharito watches so much video, both scouting clip packages and live games from Germany and England and Mexico—"not just watching the ball, and not just watching to enjoy the game," as he puts it. It's why he spends so many hours on the practice field, both with his team and by himself. "Of course, you need to work," he says. "For us it's an education every day. You can always learn something new from football. If a player starts thinking they don't need to learn, they are dead."

ONE OF THE BIGGEST MISCONCEPTIONS about soccer is that, unlike other sports, such as American football or basketball, there are no designed plays during the run of play. I can't tell you how many times over the years I have been lectured—usually by a so-called soccer "mastermind" from Europe—that Americans struggle at the world's most popular sport because we're conditioned by our culture "to do what you're told by the coach," military-style, on designed plays in American football and basketball, instead of showing the self-taught creativity that's found in soccer.

This is nonsense on multiple levels. For one thing, the most popular U.S. pro team sports feature plenty of creativity, especially basketball, in which players are given the freedom to improvise within the framework of a designed play and often ignore the coach's instructions altogether. What's more, the idea that soccer has no designed plays simply isn't true. Obviously, there are choreographed sequences on dead-ball situations—set plays—which are drawing more attention than ever from soccer's data analysts as a way to maximize goal-scoring chances from free kicks near the box. (Atlético Madrid has made a science of scoring on set plays under manager Diego Simeone, while the 2015–16 Danish league champion, Midtjylland, even hired a former NFL player to come work with the team on creative set pieces.)

But even during the run of play, many of the world's top soccer teams design and execute systematized patterns that have a framework not unlike what we see in an NBA half-court offense. These patterns appear most often in club soccer, in which the players are together year-round and have the time to work on perfecting their timing and understanding of each other's tendencies. But some national teams run patterns as well, including Mexico under Juan Carlos Osorio. "I love basketball," Osorio tells me. "I can see so many movements, and they specifically have many patterns where if they want the ball to be with the point guard or a playmaker, they will synchronize the movements and the right player will end up with the ball."

And so Osorio has designed patterns with the objective of increasing the chances that Chicharito receives a ball in the box with the opportunity to score a goal. How does Osorio do this? For starters, the Colombian manager is fascinated by the scientific study of the human brain and its applications to his players. During my two days with the Mexican team, Osorio instructs one of his assistants, Jorge Enrique Ríos Duque, to show me *The Brain*, a program produced by the History Channel that details how the brain functions in elite team sports and in other human contexts. The program, which Osorio has shown to all his Mexican players, includes scenes of Cirque du Soleil members in a discussion of kinetic intelligence; of the former major league baseball player Shelley Duncan saying 90 percent of elite sports is mental; and of a former concert pianist with Alzheimer's disease who's still able to play complex tunes because they are part of his brain's procedural memory.

"My father was diagnosed with Alzheimer's," Osorio says. "I go and play billiards with him. He's 86, so now he doesn't have the ability or accuracy, but when he sees something, I tell him, 'What are you going to do?' He says, 'I'm going to hit this ball into this side, and it's going to take this turn or movement.' He knows. That's procedural memory. How we shave in the morning. How we walk. How we ride a bicycle. How you drive. How you play a football match.'"

Osorio says he uses every training session to model game situations with the patterns he has developed for the team, so that they become second nature to his players. If they go through the same framework 10 to 15 times in every practice, Osorio argues, they will do it right sometimes and wrong at other times. But that repetition will eventually cause them to store the information in their brains' procedural memory. "The training has to be real-game situations," he says. "It has to be specific, and it has to be down to the smallest details. You have to synchronize all those movements. We try to create patterns. We love to play offensive football, enjoyable football, so we want to bring the ball from the back. And we need patterns. Patterns to bring it from the defensive third into the middle third. Now we improve that and try to have patterns to bring it from the middle third into the offensive third."

Part of Osorio's instructions for his Mexican attackers involves putting themselves in specific zones on the field. "We use the natural lines on the field," he says, "to try and create an understanding of where everybody has to run, including the striker, when the ball is in certain positions."

Take crosses, for example. Based on research of the English Premier League, Osorio says, more than 50 percent of the crosses that result in a goal come from a 10-by-14-meter zone coming out from either far corner of the penalty box. That's where he wants his team's crosses to originate. As for the striker on the end of those crosses, Osorio wants him to be stationed in what he calls the "second 6-yard box"—a zone that can be imagined if you take the existing 6-yard box and move it out 6 more yards from the goal, so that line includes the penalty spot (which is 12 yards from the goal line). He can run to either the near post or the far post, but if the striker is in the second 6-yard box, Osorio reasons, the cross is more likely to reach him without being picked off by the goalkeeper coming off his line.

"We try to get our attackers to go to specific areas to play our percentages, as opposed to just leaving it to the creativity of the players," Osorio explains. "We do have very creative players, and we encourage them to play to their abilities, but we also understand it's very important that we have certain patterns to at least have good points of reference for all the strikers to move to."

Osorio has several solid strikers at his disposal, including Carlos Vela, Giovani Dos Santos, Raúl Jiménez, Marco Fabián, and Oribe Peralta. But his first choice for the lone centerforward position in his 4-3-3 formation is Chicharito. That doesn't mean Hernández starts every game—Osorio is famous for his rotation policy, in which he makes anywhere from two to eight changes in the lineup for each game—but if Mexico is in a must-win situation, you can be safe assuming Chicharito will be on the field. "If I compare Javier with other great goal scorers, there are certain things that are common to all of them," Osorio says. "One, he has a knack for the goal. Sometimes it seems like every rebound or every deflection goes into his path. Another thing is he doesn't dwell on a missed opportunity. He always looks forward to the next one. He has good ability in the air. He has good pace, and he makes those diagonal runs starting from the first defender in behind the second one. He also has the willingness to work defensively."

How do Osorio's designed attacking patterns work with Chicharito and the rest of his Mexican teammates? In Denver, the two men sit down together with me and explain the details of two different examples of *El Tri*'s synchronization.

SYNCHRONIZATION NUMBER 1
USING CHICHARITO AS A SURPRISE LEFT-WINGER

In Mexico's World Cup qualifier at home against Costa Rica on March 24, 2017, Osorio pulled a huge surprise on the *Ticos*, moving Hernández away from his customary centerforward position and starting him instead on the left wing of Mexico's front three. Target man Oribe Peralta got the call in the centerforward spot. Osorio trained his players in the new setup every day in the week leading up to the game, and Chicharito was encouraged by how many scoring chances they created for him in practice. But he had no idea the plan would work so well in the game, with the designed pattern setting up his eighth-minute goal, just as they had drawn it up on the tactical board. Hernández's finish, in which he one-timed Vela's pinpoint pass just a moment before being cleaned out by onrushing Costa Rican goalkeeper

Keylor Navas, was a thing of beauty. But there was a richly choreographed process that led up to it.

Sitting above the table where the manager has laid out 11 green circular tabs (for Mexico) and 11 red tabs (for Costa Rica) in their teams' respective formations—4-3-3 for Mexico, 5-4-1 for Costa Rica—Osorio and Chicharito take turns moving the puzzle pieces and explaining how their team's synchronization patterns worked that night on the first goal of Mexico's 2–0 victory.

The keys to the goal lay in several elements: surprise, numerical advantage, the synchronization of the Mexican attackers, and the creation of doubts in opposing defenders. The surprise comes from deploying Chicharito on the left wing and a centerforward of a completely different profile—Peralta, a target man. As Osorio notes, "These three guys [the Costa Rican centerbacks] were waiting for Javier to be here [in the box as a centerforward]. Once they saw him here [on the left wing] they are thinking, *Who's going to take him?*" Osorio compounds Costa Rica's problems by creating a tactical numerical advantage in the central midfield, where Mexico has three players to the *Ticos'* two. In cases of numerical advantage, obviously, one attacker is always going to be open and defenders will be forced to engage with one or hedge and be caught in the middle, neither of which is an optimal defensive situation.

Osorio designs a synchronized movement by his players to maximize the leverage of these advantages. When Mexico advances toward midfield with the ball, Peralta retreats from his advanced centerforward position toward midfield, dragging his defender with him and creating open space for Chicharito to run into from the left wing. Due to Mexico's numerical advantage, Costa Rican right centerback Johnny Acosta will be forced to decide whether to mark Chicharito or midfielder Jonathan Dos Santos. "We wanted to create doubts—with me especially," Hernández says, "because that was the idea of the movement. [Acosta] has a *doubt* with Jonathan. And that's what happened. It was the thing that we practiced in training."

"Javier wisely used the proper word—*doubts*," Osorio says. "That's what we try to create." The presence of Dos Santos draws Acosta, who thinks he can intercept a potential pass to Dos Santos, but that leaves Chicharito open. "So the ball goes over to Javier," Osorio says. "We call this *synchronization*. Because when [Jonathan] comes forward, Javier has to run, and how do we know that? When we get [centerback Héctor Moreno] on the ball and he moves the ball forward. He's looking for a pass."

Hernández flashes a grin. "Synchronization!"

March 24, 2017: Mexico–Costa Rica. The design of Synchronization No. 1, with Chicharito as a surprise left winger.

While Moreno passes to Araujo, centerforward Peralta retreats toward center circle, dragging his defender with him to create space in front of the goal.

Araujo passes to Peralta as Costa Rica's back line advances forward. Chicharito lurks out to the left, offside for now.

With his back to the goal, Peralta controls the ball and lays it off to right winger Vela. Meanwhile, Costa Rican defender Acosta has doubts over whether to mark Chicharito or Dos Santos.

With Costa Rica's back line retreating (to bring Chicharito onside), Vela advances and fires a pass to Chicharito, who cuts diagonally into the box and shoots past Navas for a 1–0 lead.

Watching the passing sequence that leads to Chicharito's goal on video, you marvel at the fluid movements within the structure that Osorio has laid out. Deep in Mexico's defensive half, Moreno starts everything with a diagonal pass forward to the right centerback Néstor Araujo, who approaches the edge of the center circle unmarked. Costa Rica, packing things in at Estadio Azteca, is applying no defensive pressure in that part of the field. Araujo could pass the ball centrally to defensive midfielder Rafa Márquez, but Costa Rican forward Johan Venegas has dropped back to cover Márquez, who's looking at Araujo and pointing at the open passing lane farther up the middle of the field.

Araujo sees it. Per Osorio's instructions, the centerforward, Peralta, has dropped deep as a target man, dragging the middle centerback (Giancarlo González) with him and leaving all sorts of open space upfield in the middle of the penalty box. That's critical in the design of the play. Araujo rifles a right-footed pass 25 yards on the ground to Peralta, bypassing Mexico's three central midfielders and breaking Costa Rica's defensive lines. González is in tight on Peralta, whose back is to the goal 45 yards away. Peralta's first touch on the hot pass isn't perfect—he pops it up a couple feet above his head—but Peralta uses his body to keep González at bay, then turns to his left (Mexico's right attacking side) and hits a pass to right-winger Vela running 5 yards ahead in the channel between Francisco Calvo (the left centerback) and Ronald Matarrita (the left wingback).

At this point, Chicharito is simply watching the play unfold, standing on the left side in a position that's 2 yards offside. Costa Rica's right wingback Cristian Gamboa is a couple yards away, while *Tico* right centerback Johnny Acosta is in no-man's-land, marking neither Chicharito (open 5 yards away and behind him) nor midfielder Jonathan Dos Santos (open 10 yards away in front of him). *This* is the exact doubt that Osorio wanted to create in Acosta: *Which player do I mark?* Six minutes into the game, Mexico has already surprised Costa Rica by putting Chicharito on the left side and a retreating target man as the centerforward, and now *El Tri* is compounding the uncertainty for Acosta. The advantage that Mexico has created is even more impressive considering that Costa Rica—a World Cup 2014 quarterfinalist that advanced from a group that included Italy, England, and Uruguay—is parking the bus and deploying its tried-and-true, deeply conservative *five-man back line*.

Let's shift our focus back to Vela and the ball. Osorio likes to use Vela as an inverted winger, a player whose dominant foot is the opposite of the side he's playing on. As a left-footed attacker on the right wing, Vela rarely stays wide and hits crosses with his weaker right foot, but he often cuts inside to create danger centrally. When he receives the pass from Peralta, Vela has options. If he were a right-footed player, he'd probably try to blast through the channel between Calvo and Matarrita and shoot on goal. Instead, Vela takes his first touch with his trusty left foot and stops on a dime. The move creates a pocket of space between Vela and his two defenders, who have retreated at speed on the right—conveniently rendering Chicharito *onside* on the left 20 yards away.

Hernández has just started his run, and there is nothing but wide-open green grass between him and the goalkeeper, Navas, 28 yards away. Because Peralta retreated from the centerforward position, the middle centerback, González—who's supposed to be the rock of the Costa Rican back line—is 7 yards behind Vela and desperately trying to close ground on him. If anyone is going to stop Vela's pass, it will be González. But Vela is too quick in thought and action, and he jabs a left-footed pass on the ground into the penalty box, right in the path of Chicharito's run. The only question now is whether goalkeeper Navas, who has taken off from his 6-yard box the moment after Vela released the pass, will get to the ball before Hernández does.

Navas fails. Chicharito meets the ball 13 yards out and chips a right-footed shot over Navas, who's sliding into the Mexican like a baseball player trying to break up a double play. By the time the ball hits the back of the net, Hernández's momentum has carried him 8 more yards ahead and he's flat on his stomach inside the 6-yard box. The look on Chicharito's face as he celebrates with his teammates—and as the old ThunderDome stadium erupts with noise—is priceless. It's as though he's screaming: *Can you believe it worked just like we drew it up? Can you really believe it?*

Design matters. Craft matters. Patterns matter.

All told, the sequence from Moreno's pass deep in Mexico's own end to Chicharito's goal has involved five players, four passes, and just 11 seconds of elapsed time. Viewed at full speed, it's a brilliant execution of synchronization.

SYNCHRONIZATION NUMBER 2
USING CHICHARITO AS A CENTERFORWARD AND MAXIMIZING THE FULL WIDTH OF THE ATTACKING THIRD

Most of the time in Osorio's 4-3-3 formation, Hernández will be playing as the centerforward, not as a left-winger. And the manager has patterns designed for that situation, too, usually against a more common 4-4-2 opposition alignment, in which the actions depend in part on whether Mexico's wingers are natural (that is, having their dominant foot on the side they're playing) or inverted.

Osorio rearranges the 22 green and red circular tabs on the table below us. "We're playing now with natural wingers," he says by way of starting. "Let's say this is Jürgen Damm [on the right wing]. He's not coming inside because he doesn't have a left foot. He wants to produce a cross with the right foot." In that case, Osorio instructs Hernández to make a near-post run for Damm's cross while ensuring that Damm (outside the box) and Hernández (in the second six-yard box) are in the zones on the field that Osorio wants his players to be in to increase their chances of scoring on a cross.

If the right-winger with the ball is inverted—if it's a left-footed player like Vela or Giovani Dos Santos—Osorio asks the winger to cut inside, where the manager gives his attackers more options within his framework. The first option is to look for a pass to Chicharito if the striker decides to make a ball-side run behind the back line, whereupon they'll work a give-and-go as Chicharito returns the pass to the winger, continuing to cut into the box. If that doesn't happen, Osorio asks Hernández to move a couple yards closer to the goal. If the centerbacks go with him, fine. If they don't, it's no problem if Chicharito is in an offside position, because he's not the immediate target of the pass from the winger.

Instead, Osorio wants the opposite-side fullback to make a bombing run (in this case, up the left sideline) to receive a pass over the top from the right-winger who has cut inside. "The pass goes to the left back because he's not offside," Osorio says. "That's a very, very critical point." Once the left back receives the ball in that spot, he has options: Send a cross to centerforward

If Mexico uses a natural winger (the right-footed Damm), Damm is asked to advance down the flank and deliver a cross to Chicharito, with both players located in the high-scoring-percentage zones preferred by Osorio.

If Mexico uses an inverted winger (the left-footed Vela), Vela is asked to cut inside with the ball and look to make a pass to Chicharito making a diagonal run across the box. Once Chicharito receives the ball, he can shoot or work a give-and-go with Vela.

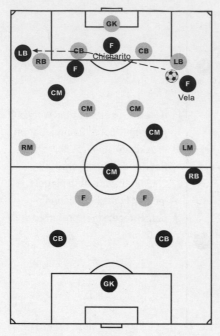

Instead of passing to Chicharito, Vela can send a pass over the top to the left back, who has advanced far upfield in the attack.

Once the left back has the ball, he has multiple attacking choices—three passing options and the dribble—with a numerical advantage on the defensive team. (All of these diagrams can apply to the other side of the field as well.)

Chicharito (who will almost certainly be onside now because of the retreating centerbacks); cross to an attacking midfielder who has also run into the box; unspool a short pass in to the left-winger who has cut into the box; or use Mexico's numerical advantage to try to create something on the dribble moving toward the goal.

Osorio says he got the idea for the pattern and synchronization in part from listening to Mexican defender Diego Reyes (formerly with the Spanish club Espanyol) tell him about the challenges of defending against the world's best front three in recent years: Barcelona's nominal wingers Lionel Messi and Neymar and centerforward Luis Suárez. "I love talking to my players," Osorio explains. "Diego Reyes, playing for Espanyol versus Barcelona, told me the most difficult part was playing against Suárez here because they have this play. This is Messi [cutting in from the right wing with the ball on his left foot]. He can take the whole team on if he wants. Suárez could be offside, because the ball is not going to play to him. This is Neymar [on the left wing]. Neymar comes in here [to the penalty box] and brings his defender here, and this is Jordi Alba [racing up the sideline from his left back position]. So *that's* the ball that they are looking for."

"Exactly," Chicharito says. "The thing is, [Reyes] said the most difficult thing is not marking Suárez on *this* ball [at the start of the play], it's on the *other* one [coming from Alba on the left]. With this ball and the numbers, he said, how are you going to defend it? Because [Suárez] has the advantage in front of the goal, and with just one pass he can score."

As Chicharito speaks, Osorio sits back and observes his star forward, a smile creasing the manager's face. It's one thing for a group of players to execute a synchronization on the field, but Hernández's ability to verbalize exactly what is supposed to happen—in his second language, no less—shows an even higher level of understanding. It reveals a granular awareness of what every Mexican player on the field needs to be doing to make the coordinated play work. "When the ball comes here [to the left back], *synchronize it*," Chicharito says. "We need to synchronize this movement. Only one guy in the world [Messi] can take on all 11 players. But the other ones, we need to think more. The synchronization that [Osorio] is telling you about—imagine all the movements, but if one defender blocks this, it changes everything. So you need to improvise. That's football sometimes as well. You need to think *before* you have the ball, *when* you have the ball, and *after* you pass the ball. Because the ball is not stopping! And you need to keep thinking. That's why he's making the synchronization—to make something *without* thinking. Just to know it more naturally."

With the tag team of Hernández and Osorio, one man's energy feeds off that of the other. Osorio becomes so engrossed in the conversation that he ends up being nearly an hour late to his own coaches' meeting. It doesn't matter. When one of his assistants approaches to spirit him away, Osorio happily waves him off. "I am learning a lot here!" he says in Spanish. The manager still has a smile on his face after hearing Hernández go into so much detail explaining what Osorio has been trying to do with the team.

"Fantastic," Osorio finally says. "I didn't know he knew so much."

⬠ ⬠ ⬠

So much about the forward position is connected to confidence and emotions. You can't get too high or too low, Hernández maintains, but goals are so hard to come by that it's no wonder strikers whipsaw between mental extremes more than any other kind of field player. Yet there are other major factors that can influence a player's emotions, and foremost among them is playing time. Over my two days embedded with the Mexican men's national team, one of my main challenges is to understand Osorio's rotation system—his policy of making wholesale changes to the starting lineup nearly every game—and how Hernández and the Mexican players respond to it.

Osorio's rotations drive large sections of Mexico's fans and media nuts. *How can you make eight changes between the first two games of the Confederations Cup? Why would you prevent the same four-man back line from getting used to playing together every game? How can you leave out your best goal scorer?* "They say, 'Hey, why would you do that?'" says Osorio. "They want to play with the same 11 against Croatia, an aerial game, as against Chile, a possession game. They want to play a defensive game against Brazil and a very offensive game against El Salvador. But our proposition is that we try to play the same type of football with different levels. So if we play Croatia or the USA, we need to have five good headers of the ball because Croatia and the USA are very good on set pieces. That's my responsibility: Who can have a good aerial game but also play good football in our system?"

Not even Chicharito is exempted from Osorio's rotations, even in games that matter. A few days after our joint interview, Hernández will be left out of the starting lineup in a home World Cup qualifier against Honduras. He won't even come off the bench in *El Tri*'s 3–0 victory, and he will have no problem with the situation. The same thing will happen a couple weeks later in Mexico's second game of the Confederations Cup, which it will win 2–1, with some difficulty, against New Zealand.

Chicharito won't complain, and when we sit down together he leans forward in his chair and makes himself explicitly clear. Hernández wants Osorio, who's sitting right next to him, to hear this. He wants Mexico's passionate and ever-demanding fans to hear this. And he most definitely wants Mexico's media to hear this. The message from Chicharito: Lay off Osorio. This man from Colombia is doing something special, something that can take Mexico to soccer heights it has never reached before. This man from Colombia has the Mexican players competing as a team, trusting one another and their coach, even if he changes the starting lineup with regularity. This man from Colombia has connected with his players, not just in the granular details of soccer but in the deepest of emotional ways, too.

"I feel empathy with him because he has been very criticized and very judged by a lot of people, without even having the chance to prove himself," Hernández says, looking over at Osorio. "What he's doing [with Mexico] is more than football, and that's the most important thing. That's what the top clubs and national teams have. And that's why they are world champions. If we want to get there, to dream about that and go in that path, we need to do that as well."

Chicharito tells a story. When he first met Osorio, after a Champions League game in October 2015, Osorio asked his star about what he thought made Sir Alex Ferguson, his former manager at Manchester United, such a remarkable figure. Hernández told Osorio that Ferguson had a gift. A club squad has more than two dozen players, but only 11 will start in a game. Seven will be on the bench, and all the other players on the roster will be left out entirely. And yet somehow, Chicharito told him, Ferguson was able to keep the majority of his players happy "instead of the opposite that sometimes happens."

Nearly two years later, Hernández says, Osorio is doing the same thing with Mexico. "He's making the Mexican players understand why. The *why* of everything," Chicharito says. "If I'm going to play, if he's going to play over me, you understand why. A lot of coaches, they just say, 'You are not going to play,' or they tell you lies. He has the thing that a lot of these people don't have: the listening. The difficult thing that he does is he goes and speaks with you, to hear what the player can say. So that's something that is good.

"You can tell him sometimes, 'Hey, trainer, I'm playing like s— because in my personal life I'm in a mess right now.' Or you can say, 'Hey, trainer, I don't feel like you can trust in me.' But you can say it in a personal chat. Sometimes, with a head coach, you can't say the things you want to say because he can take it bad. [Osorio] is creating that [trust]."

Hernández is on one of his high-energy verbal riffs, the kind where he can speak feverishly for seven minutes without stopping. When the man says he's hyperactive, he does not lie. But there is more than quantity to what Chicharito is saying here. His candor borders on the astonishing. Osorio, sitting right next to him, is silent. Even he seems surprised by what Chicharito is revealing. "I can speak about my teammates, because I've been with them almost 10 years," Hernández says. "We're here now playing in almost our third World Cup. But I feel something completely new. Everybody is happier. We want to train. We like to train. When he came, he put in his idea about rotation. It's not easy. Everybody wants to play. There are some players that are almost Man of the Match, then in the next game he decides to give him a rest or play another player. It's *not* easy."

But this is part of the plan, Chicharito says. The plan that he thinks could take Mexico all the way to a World Cup title. "He's making something different, not only for Juan Carlos Osorio, but he's making it for Mexico," Hernández says. "He believes in the potential that we've got. Unfortunately, in our country it's difficult culturally for us to speak good about other people. We always have that feeling of, 'I'm better than him. I deserve better things than him.' That's something about our country to change. And he's changing it. If I'm not playing, it's because it's his decision. You need to respect that and say, 'Hey, I'm going to be ready.' He never makes you feel like you're not playing because you don't deserve it or you're not good enough. So that's something in your mind that you can manage better."

Mexico has gone out in the Round of 16 in the last six World Cups. But in Chicharito's mind, Mexico should strive not just to compete to win World Cups, but to do so on a regular basis. "We want to make that normal, like Germany does, like Brazil," he says. "Even you guys in the USA, you want that. We want to keep that, and that's what he's creating: a good culture." And if the biggest star on the team buys into that approach publicly and privately, chances are that the rest of the Mexican players will, too.

We already know from our earlier discussion that Osorio is obsessed with tactics, and over our two days together he shows exactly how detail-oriented he is. At one point, he shows me an ordinary-looking binder with laminated sheets of paper inside.

"This is all tactics," he says. "Everything that I believe in the game is here." Inside are several things: Osorio's favorite training session plans, meticulously drawn out in black, pink, and light-blue ink; his calendar, also color-coded, with plans for what he wants to do each day; and right there, in plain words, a page that lays out a philosophy.

"I admire [Marcelo] Bielsa, [Pep] Guardiola, and [Sir Alex] Ferguson," says Osorio, who has printed out Guardiola's principles of the game. "So Guardiola says, principle number one: the risk of always attacking. The open man is the key to keeping possession. You always have to find the opening. The next passing lane is the open man. The third man gives depth. So if I play to you and you back to me, the depth is given by the guy who is running forward. The intention of moving the ball is not to move the ball. It is to move the opposition. And finally: Always try to play in between the lines. So this risk of playing man to man, we'll take that. It's very risky, but we'll do it." At his training sessions, Osorio insists on laying out the cones himself. One morning, he spends nearly an hour with his staff dissecting video from a friendly against Croatia and debating whether or not they should have a one-man wall or no wall at all on free kicks from distance that can't be shot on goal.

Osorio's fascination with the brain isn't just tied to wiring his players' procedural memory so they'll know his tactics and synchronization patterns on the field as second nature. In the wake of Mexico's 7–0 loss to Chile in the 2016 Copa América Centenario—a crushing defeat that nearly cost Osorio his job—his study of the brain convinced him that his Mexican players were part of a classic fight-or-flight situation. "Basically, the one part of the brain that has not progressed in the last million years or more is the reptilian brain, the one that's in charge of survival," Osorio says. "It's a primitive instinct. When you are driving at night and the lights of the car hit on the deer, it stays put. Because it's paralyzed. It's in shock. That's the reptilian brain. And it also happens in sports. They shut down and cannot react and look petrified. That's what happened in [the 7–0 loss to Chile]. I am the first one to confess. I had never lost by more than three goals. I thought it would never happen. But I felt almost paralyzed. I had no Plan B. Now we do, because from that experience we have learned so much. Now we have Plan B and even Plan C. We know how to react."

After his summer of reflection, Osorio came away valuing his players' emotions more than he ever had in his 17-year coaching career. If his players' mentality isn't stable, he argues, that deficit will register on and off the field. He refers back to the History Channel program, *The Brain*, that he shows all his players. "How do we deal with those emotions?" he asks. "And if we really believe in that, we talk about the amygdala and the limbic system. Some people say, 'That's crazy. That has nothing to do with football!' But it does. That's where previous information and memory connect with the emotions." Osorio uses as an example a defender who on a previous play wasn't able to make a controlled run and pass out of the back. If the situation presents itself again, Osorio says, that player is much more likely just to boot the ball clear out of the back (and give up possession to the other team).

"Most coaches prefer not to even bother reading about the mind, the brain, and the emotions, and just say, 'Football is football, it's just a game,'" Osorio says. "But at the end of the day, it's a game played by human beings full of emotions. And those emotions are [feeding] the decisions that they take in the game. A lot of people talk about emotions and character and conviction and personality like it was something really easy to understand. And it's the most difficult part to understand in any human being, never mind an athlete with his heart running at 190 beats per minute and thinking, 'If I lose this game, then I'm going to lose my job and my family is going to be in a really vulnerable position.' It's crucial to understand."

Osorio's approach with his Mexico team has resonated with Chicharito, who has achieved at the highest levels of the club game and wants to see Mexico get there at the international level. "Of course, he has his ideas about football, and we can't forget that we are playing football," Hernández says. "But we are also human beings, you know? We aren't robots. Of course, he wants to win. I want to win. I want to score goals. He wants to look at me scoring goals. He wants to make Mexico champions of the world. That's normal. But the best thing is that he wants to make the players better. To make me one step better. To make my teammates one step better. Imagine: With 23 players getting better like that, we're going to make a lot of progress."

One of the changes Osorio made after the 7–0 Chile loss was to bring onto his staff Imanol Ibarrondo as Mexico's new mental coach. A Basque Spaniard from Bilbao, Ibarrondo has kind eyes, an easy smile, and the gray beard and casual but stylish wardrobe that might be worn by a chef whose restaurant has three Michelin stars. "My work is a job of accompaniment," Ibarrondo says in Spanish. "I accompany others and help them transform themselves, to help convert them into people who deserve extraordinary results. This requires a process of change and transformation. It requires that players and teams take consciousness

of what they're doing, thinking, and feeling—of their relationships and conversations. Of their connections that are important for the team." Ibarrondo played in the Spanish first division
for Rayo Vallecano. In his book, *La primera vez que la pegué con la
izquierda* (*The First Time That I Kicked It with My Left Foot*), the first
story he tells is about a game in which his Rayo team lost 7–0
to Barcelona in the Camp Nou. "When [Osorio] read this," Ibarrondo says, "he saw someone who might be able to understand
and help."

Osorio invited Ibarrondo to spend a week with him and his
staff in Mexico in October 2016. They spent hours talking about
leadership and connection, and then Osorio asked the Spaniard
to come to Columbus, Ohio, with the team in advance of their
World Cup qualifier against the United States in November. Columbus had taken on mythic significance for both teams after
the U.S. had beaten Mexico four straight times there by the same
2–0 scoreline. On a famous night for Mexican soccer, *El Tri* ended
the Columbus hex, beating the U.S. 2–1 on Rafa Márquez's late
set-piece goal. Ibarrondo takes great pains to give the credit for
that victory to Osorio, for daring his team to be the attacking
protagonist and developing a game plan to leverage Mexico's
technical advantages, while limiting the U.S.'s set-piece threat.

But in the days before that game, Ibarrondo helped lay the
groundwork, too, with the Mexican players. "I worked above all
on the idea that we're creating a new history for the Mexican
national team," he says. "We worked hard on their connections,
having more conversations with each other, sharing their fears
but also their desires. This creates a lot of connection, and that
showed on the field. And the rest? I believe sometimes the uni-

verse works in your favor if you do things the right way." Through that success against the U.S., and through his individual and group sessions with the Mexican players and staff, Ibarrondo won everyone over. After the U.S. game, Osorio hired him on a long-term basis through World Cup 2018.

Osorio is well aware of the old stereotype of Mexican players: that they are often supremely talented and technically skilled, but they aren't mentally strong enough when it matters the most. But he doesn't buy it. "Various Latin countries all say the same," Osorio says. "The Peruvians say, 'We have very talented players, but we drink too much.' The Colombians: 'We are very talented, but it is too easy here. We are always in the comfort zone.' The Ecuadorians say the same. Even the Brazilians at a certain point. When I coached at São Paulo, they said, 'There are great footballers here, but their mentality isn't strong enough.' We came to the conclusion that it has a lot to do with culture and who can conquer us. The Mexicans are very similar to Colombians, Peruvians, and Ecuadorians. It's like we believe we have great talent but we can't learn how to compete. And that's the biggest mistake. With the proper competition, all humans can learn how to compete."

Ending the Columbus Curse against the U.S. in November 2016—in the midst of political tensions just days after Donald Trump won the U.S. presidency—was a defining accomplishment in the transformation of Osorio's Mexican team. "It had a lot to do with mentality," he says. "We approached that game with three specific things: (A) There were no political issues. It was just a sporting event. This is football. 11v11. (B) Recognize that the Americans are very athletic and very good on set pieces. Respect that. And (C) We are a good team. We can compete against them. We were focused on those three things. And I think at the end we deserved the three points against a very good U.S. team."

In Osorio's view, it's important to stay in contact with his Mexico players, both when things are going well and *especially* when things aren't going well, either with their club teams or in their personal lives. There is more to soccer, Osorio says he has learned, than the Xs and Os on his tactical board. "I look at the players, and I have to understand the emotions that go through their minds," he says, "because whether they are famous or not, whether they have money or not, whether they are younger or older, they have emotions like I do. And it's my responsibility to try to deal with those emotions, as opposed to just criticizing them."

By taking the time to listen to his players, Chicharito says, Osorio has earned their trust—and the belief that even if Hernández and other players aren't starting every game, their sacrifice is in the service of a greater team goal. Chicharito is convinced that Mexico can go further than ever before at the next World Cup, and he is sustained by what he experiences inside the Mexican team whenever it's together. You can sense the respect when Mexico's biggest star turns to his Colombian coach and says, "In this national team, now we feel open. I can feel it as well with the other players. The best thing in any sport or in any profession, and even in life, is when you meet people that can help you to get the best of you."

★ ★ ★

OVER THE YEARS, JAVIER HERNÁNDEZ has been the victim of a fallacy. Detractors have called him a "goal poacher," damning him with faint praise, as if to say he's lacking in skill. The word *poacher* is fascinating. In realms outside of soccer, *poaching* is an illegal activity—what happens when bandits encroach on private lands in a wildlife preserve to kill animals and sell them for profit elsewhere. The suggestion in soccer is that a goal poacher has committed some sort of unwritten infraction by pouncing on loose balls in the penalty box, that those goals are somehow lesser or not deserved.

This is all hogwash, of course. The greatest thing about soccer is its simplicity: A goal is a goal is a goal. Beautiful goals and ugly goals count the same. "He can finish first time like very few, but he can always score the ugly goals," Osorio says of Chicharito. "It's not just the nice goals but the ugly goals, which a lot of players are either incapable of or do not fancy doing."

Ugly goals. Few players in the modern game score ugly goals with more regularity—and, let's be honest, more satisfaction— than Hernández. Chicharito has been scoring ugly goals for so many years that it's clearly no coincidence. After hours of interviews over a two-year period, Hernández reveals something to me in Denver that he has not mentioned before. It's one thing to "smell the intuition" and run where you think your teammate might be aiming his cross. But it's another thing entirely to assume the cross is about to be misfired into a completely unintended location. "Sometimes I guess that a *bad* cross is coming," says Chicharito. "It's not easy to make 10 crosses and have 10 good ones. Not even Dani Alves or Alex Sandro or Marcelo can. They make bad crosses, and sometimes you need to expect that. That's why I score a lot of goals when the crosses are not the best ones." In some ways, ugly crosses—as long as they're not *too* ugly—give Hernández an advantage, combining with his willingness to run in the box when not every forward would do so. The result: ugly goals by the bucketload.

The term *goal poacher* is of a piece with the language of soccer. In no other sport do we hear the word *deserved* or some derivative of it as often as we do in *fútbol*. *Manchester United outshot Everton 10 to 2 and thoroughly deserved the 2–0 victory. Atlético Madrid stole three points at Barcelona by converting a stoppage-time set piece to win after being dominated in possession.* Deflected shots that turn into goals are usually greeted with a tsk-tsk for those who benefit from them. We journalists love to ask after the game if a player "was trying" to score the goal that might have been an attempted pass, the implication being that we'll view it with lower regard if that isn't the case. Players are well aware of this, naturally—see Ronaldinho's famous 40-yard goal over the head of England goalkeeper David Seaman in the World Cup 2002 quarterfinals—so they *always* say they were trying to score, even if they weren't. On a case-by-case basis, the whole "intention" discussion makes sense, though. It's like not calling your shot on the pool table.

Yet *poacher* may be the most unfair word in soccer's strain of merit-based language, precisely because to acquire the reputation of a poacher means you have to be scoring goals—the hardest thing to do in the sport—*on a regular basis*. The repeatability of the so-called poacher's success over a long period means that, by definition, we are not talking about luck or coincidence. Being in the right place at the right time *nearly all the time* to score goals is most definitely a skill—the result of anticipation or, in Chicharito's evocative language, a smelled intuition.

Hernández says he's fully aware of the English word *poacher*—and that it's a criticism that people have often applied to him. What's his opinion of the term? He grins and leans back in his seat. "To have a good goal poacher, you need to have awesome midfielders, wingers, and number 10s to be there. It's part of life, not only in my profession, that there is always going to be a *but*. But . . . *this*. But . . . *that*. *Only a goal poacher*. Some people want to say that takes credit away from me. *He's only there poaching balls. It's easy*."

But if it were easy to be a goal poacher, then every forward would do that. The truth is that not every forward wants to do the dirty work that's often required in the pursuit of ugly goals. For a decade, Chicharito has been willing and able to do so. For Hernández, ugly goals have become a thing of beauty. "Very few have that quality," says Osorio in defense of his striker. "Those who say, 'Oh, he's just a goal poacher,' either they are envious or they don't understand the game. That's a talent, like being an athlete is a talent, like being good in the air is a talent. Being a goal poacher, having a knack for the goal, that's a talent that many would like to have, and very few have."

What's more, the data shows that Chicharito is not an extreme poacher, if we take *poacher* to mean a player who has a lack of involvement in the game outside of goal scoring. As the analyst Ben Torvaney notes, using Opta data, if we take the same top 10 producers of expected goals in the Premier League from 2010–11 to 2016–17 shown earlier in this chapter, Chicharito's successful passes in the final third of the field are significantly fewer than those of Luis Suárez, Sergio Agüero, and Dimitar Berbatov, but they're not remarkably low.

PLAYER	GOALS	xG	xG/SHOT	SHOTS	FINAL-THIRD PASSES
Sergio Agüero	0.74	0.61	0.13	4.9	4.9
Edin Džeko	0.62	0.59	0.13	4.6	9.2
Robin van Persie	0.64	0.57	0.14	4.2	10.2
Mario Balotelli	0.40	0.55	0.11	5.0	9.0
Luis Suárez	0.63	0.53	0.11	4.9	15.0
Javier Hernández	0.60	0.52	0.18	2.9	8.6
Daniel Sturridge	0.61	0.50	0.12	4.3	9.4
Papiss Demba Cissé	0.52	0.49	0.16	3.0	6.0
Dimitar Berbatov	0.57	0.49	0.16	3.1	12.7
Harry Kane	0.66	0.48	0.12	4.1	9.3

SOURCE: OPTA

Here Chicharito takes the conversation in a direction that I don't expect, comparing the differences in the expectations for him from his coaches and teammates at Manchester United, Real Madrid, and Bayer Leverkusen over the years. To hear Hernández analyze it, there is a difference between movement inside the penalty box and movement—mobility, in this case—to take himself outside the penalty box. At Manchester United, nobody was asking him to spend time outside the box. "Sometimes I watch my games," he says. "I played completely different in my years at United than at Real Madrid and at Leverkusen in the same position. How? Because at United I don't need to move [outside the box] and I don't need to run. I have [wide players Ryan] Giggs, [Antonio] Valencia, Nani, Ji-Sung Park in my first years. I can be here [in the box]. They pass to [central midfielder Paul] Scholes. I do a movement, Scholes and [Michael] Carrick put the ball here and I score goals. Then you have [forward] Wayne Rooney doing Wayne Rooney things or [Dimitar] Berbatov doing Berbatov things. I'm going to take advantage of my role and what I need to do. If he's doing this, if he's doing that, I want to be here and I score the goals."

At Real Madrid, the team usually played with a front three instead of Man United's two-man front line. "And we had Cristiano Ronaldo as well," Hernández says. "They loved to go in the box, so you need to move sometimes [outside the box], expecting that he's doing the movement that you're supposed to do. So I was going a little more deep. Then at Bayer Leverkusen, the trainer there was Roger Schmidt, and he loved constantly pressuring. Pressure-pressure-pressure. So it was more direct. *Ting! Ting! Ting! Ting!* That's the sound. Pressure, recover, and boom! We played with two strikers sometimes. I was the main striker, but sometimes when I play with [Stefan] Kiessling, with Joel Pohjanpalo now, they're more box players, and I feel I know how to play outside the box, too." As a result, Hernández says, he scored more goals at Leverkusen from outside the penalty box and delivered more crosses than he ever did at Man United or Real Madrid.

You do what is asked of you, Chicharito says by way of concluding. He has different roles as a forward, depending on the team. He has proven himself adept at many of those roles, including pouncing on loose balls in the box to score. They may be ugly goals sometimes, but they are his lifeblood, and he is deeply proud of that.

"Yes, I am a goal poacher," Hernández says, embracing that loaded phrase, taking ownership of what it really means. "Yes, it could be one of my qualities."

3

THE DEFENDER

Vincent Kompany's Centerback Confidential

THE SCENE UNFOLDING ON THE GIANT SCREEN IN MANchester City's video theater is a defender's most chilling nightmare. Barcelona's Lionel Messi, the best soccer player in the world, is charging with the ball on his magical left foot toward Vincent Kompany in a Champions League game. It's a one-on-one battle, and there's nobody behind Kompany except his goalkeeper 50 yards away. How did they get here? Well, Messi received the ball 10 yards inside his own half on the right side. City is deploying a high back line, and Kompany is positioned just inside his defensive half only 20 yards away from Messi. Fernandinho, City's defensive midfielder, is out of position; Messi has already left him in his dust. When Messi sees so much open space, he almost always has one scorched-earth solution: Dribble straight toward the goal and beat everyone in his path.

It's as though Messi's left foot can charm snakes. In three

touches—all with his left foot—he turns and accelerates to top speed. The play develops quickly, but Kompany is ready. Instead of just standing and waiting for Messi, Kompany advances toward him with three steps of his own. "This is the hardest," Kompany says, watching the screen. "He's coming at full pace against you. You're stuck, and you know that if he passes you, he's gone."

But then something remarkable happens. Just when Messi cuts hard to his right and you think he's about to posterize Kompany, like so many other defenders who have been clowned in Messi's Greatest Hits, Big Vince jab-steps to his left and thrusts his right leg across his body into the path of soccer's Tasmanian devil. For some defenders against Messi, this tactic might be as useless as trying to jam a toothpick into a jet engine. But Kompany picks the ball clean off Messi with his right foot. Messi's momentum causes him to tumble over, and City recovers the ball to move in the other direction.

"That's a good intervention," Kompany says, which—considering this is Lionel Freaking Messi—is putting it mildly. Would drawing a yellow card in that situation have been worth it if he hadn't gotten all ball? "In this situation, you take it if you need to," Kompany explains. "But that is one thing that is difficult to teach sometimes. You stick your leg out at the right time, and I've been doing it since I was a kid. I love defending, and I'm passionate about it. I *hate* getting beat one-versus-one, even in training. Most of my injuries in training were because of that, because I cannot get beat. And in a game—actually in my whole career—it has happened very, very little. It doesn't matter who comes." Not even if that player is Lionel Messi.

Kompany, who's also the veteran leader of the Belgian national team, is not an ordinary Premier League player. He speaks

five languages. His father, Pierre, a former activist, left Mobu-
tu's Zaire (now the Democratic Republic of Congo) as a political refugee. His late mother, Jocelyne, was a trade union leader.
Kompany has a university degree—a rarity in European soccer,
where players turn pro as teenagers—and in December 2017 he
earned a master's in business administration at the Manchester
Business School.

It has not been an uncommon sight to see Kompany at an
MBA class the morning after playing in a Champions League
match somewhere on the Continent. Cancer claimed his mother
in 2008, and he says he found it more important than ever to
honor her wishes that he pursue his studies. There were other
reasons, too. "It was a way for me to relax, actually, in a weird
way," he says. "I have always found it important to focus on other
things, because I'm a maniac already when it comes to my game.
I live football. I breathe football. I watch football games. I needed
something to click me out of it every now and then, and it was
good for my development. It made me a more complete person."

Perhaps more than any other current soccer player, Kompany fits the term *global citizen*. "I'm not half-Belgian and half-
Congolese," Kompany once told the *New York Times*. "I'm 100
percent Belgian and 100 percent Congolese. It's a wealth I have."
With his social work for SOS Children's Villages in the DRC
and his purchase of a lower-division soccer club, BX Brussels, to
give development opportunities to young players in his hometown, it's not surprising that some observers think Kompany
could someday become an even more successful politician—if
he wishes to do so—than two former FIFA World Players of the
Year, George Weah (Liberia) and Romário (Brazil), have in their
home countries.

When he's healthy, Kompany is among the top eight center-backs in the world, a player whose impact is clear not just when he's playing but also when he has *not* been on the field for Man City, which has suffered mightily on the defensive side during his absences due to injury. What's more, Kompany studies the sport with the same keen eye and work rate that he has shown in the university classroom.

Ideas. Work. Continuing education. Those are the themes of my conversations with Kompany including about soccer and the centerback position. "I'm a football man," Kompany explains during one of our interviews at the City Football Academy in Manchester. "I consider myself a student of the game since the age of six, when I started playing. I have always had opinions and my own visions about how the game should be played, and I've always listened very carefully to managers, to the people involved in football. But at the same time, what made me improve is the fact that I can honestly say that I have changed my views so much over the years, and I'm actually proud of that. I think a lot of people in football make the mistake to stick to one philosophy because they think it defines them. And I have always been open to any new kinds of things that are available to learn."

When I started interviewing Kompany for this book, his club manager was Manuel Pellegrini, a respected Chilean who led Man City to the 2013–14 Premier League title, Kompany's second. But then something fascinating happens. Pep Guardiola, the obsessively detailed Spanish Catalan manager, joins City from Bayern Munich for the 2016–17 season. Within months, Guardiola's influence on Kompany's ongoing education is plain to anyone who listens to the captain. Kompany sounds a lot like Xabi Alonso, who had joined Guardiola's Bayern in part to prepare for a managing career. Like Alonso, who was also in his 30s, Kompany reveals that he is learning new things all the time from Guardiola, especially about the finest details of positioning on the field. It's like a PhD-level course in soccer.

"Mainly by this manager, I have been more and more convinced that this is a game of positions," Kompany says of Guardiola. "You don't want to call it a chess game, but there are similarities in the sense that players have to be really aware of where they need to stand in relation to other players at any given time on the pitch, whether that's in possession or without the ball. It's becoming more and more specific, where being a few yards too much to the left or to the right—even when you're nowhere near the ball—makes a big difference. For example, your winger coming inside too much when the ball is on the opposite side creates for the fullback who is marking [that winger] to be able to maybe mark two players from one position, because he'll be closer to your number 10 or your striker that's around. So he'll be able to provide cover for his defenders and midfielders. Whereas if you create large distances [between your winger and his teammates], the fullback can only be concerned with marking one player and can't intervene on the other one because he is farther away. He needs to take a few steps back, and so on."

Kompany is as adept at explaining the game as he is at playing it. But his most significant challenge, as he knows only too well, is staying on the field. Few top players in world soccer have been plagued by injuries more often than Kompany, who missed more than two and a half Premier League seasons between 2009 and 2018. Players with less mental fortitude would have quit the sport. Yet Kompany redoubled his efforts to play again, and he argues that the time off, while not something that he wanted, allowed him to make improvements to his game and the way he sees soccer.

"The most difficult part is the day that you get injured," he says. "For a moment your world collapses. There are a lot worse things to happen in life, but you work so hard for it. This is your reality, and when you play again is what ultimately will make you happy. So you collapse for a bit, and then in my mind I pretty quickly get back on track. I know there's a path. You speak with the doctors. They explain what you can do, and in a way I always convince myself that I can get better in that period of time. I'd rather be on the pitch with my teammates, but at the same time I get to learn about my body in ways that other people don't get a chance to do. There's no doubt that I will lack match sharpness when I come back after a long injury. But I have usually thought [so] much about how to improve my game that one kind of balances the other out. And I believe that with match sharpness I can kick on to another level."

Kompany's personal growth—a desire to always be getting better—extends to other areas, too, including his personal comportment. Losing his mother changed him, he says, as did having his own three children with his wife, Carla. "I think I have become less emotional in my game," he says. "I'm still emotional when I score a goal or I have a good tackle or an emotion over winning. But I really am appreciative of every moment more now than before, I would say. I'm a lot more calm—and in life as well. My personality has evolved on the pitch and outside the pitch."

As is the case with Alonso, I come to look forward to my conversations with Kompany with great anticipation. Here are two supremely accomplished players in the latter stages of their careers, players who could have decided there was little left for them to learn about the sport. Instead they are embracing new ideas, stepping outside their comfort zones, and spending significant time seeking to understand the methods of Guardiola, their uncompromising manager.

The protean nature of the sport energizes Kompany. "There are also the technical, tactical, and physical sides of the game that always change," he says. "Players are quicker, and some have an incredible ability to play with the left and right [feet] the same way. There are a lot of details that I have been able to witness by being at this level, and it constantly evolves."

Kompany's enthusiasm is infectious—just as it is with the best classroom teachers.

IN SOCCER, THE BATTLE FOR a header is the subject of countless classic action photographs. Muscles straining, arms stretched out like flying buttresses, opposing players leap to engage in an age-old struggle. But Kompany has a secret to share about those aerial duels. "Some strikers in England know this, but in the rest of Europe most of them don't," he says. "On any longball, people try to outjump each other. I don't mind a big jump, but to be honest, the only thing you have to do is fight for the spot where the ball is going to land. If you own that zone, it's going on your head, and you don't even need to jump."

In more than a decade as an elite centerback, Kompany has mastered so many tricks of the trade by now that he has lost count. "There are loads of things, and they become beautiful when you know them," he says. "As a defender, I can also really appreciate a good defender doing them." During one of our sessions in Manchester City's video theater, where Kompany stands in front of the giant screen and lectures me like a professor, he dives into details on some of those trade secrets. *How do you slow down a quick striker?* "If he's trying to [show for the ball] and then go deep, just let him run into you," Kompany says. "It takes a lot of energy out of his legs, he gets frustrated, and the referee usually doesn't give a foul for that." *What if that forward shakes free and tries moving past you?* Simple: "Run in his path when he's going deep."

And if the opposing team has the ball out wide, how do you decide how tightly to mark a forward in the penalty box? Begin by assessing how your teammate is marking the wide man. "One of the biggest basics that a lot of defenders get wrong is when there's pressure on the ball, you can go man-to-man on your striker," Kompany says. "*You've* got the advantage because the ball pressure means it'll be a difficult pass to play. When there's no pressure on the ball, the *striker* has the advantage because he can choose to make a run and the ball is going to come. So: Give a bit of space when there's no pressure on the ball, and close the space when there's pressure on the ball."

If you ask Kompany to describe the role of a centerback, he chooses a felicitous phrase: *Master of the castle.* As much as a team wants to attack, he says, a good defender is constantly thinking about what could happen if his teammates lose the ball. "You're always protecting the home fort, which is the goal," Kompany explains. "And I like that role. I like it when everyone's focusing on trying to score the goal, and I'm thinking ahead. Like, *He's getting the ball. What if he loses the ball? He's passed the ball. What if the guy that received the ball doesn't control the ball well?* You're always anticipating things. Sometimes you gamble, and sometimes you

have to shove people over to make sure they're in the right position. They may not understand, but you're only calling on them
to be in position—not to receive the ball, but in case we lose the
ball. That's when they can suffocate the opposing team."

One of Kompany's favorite words is *suffocate*. It's the result
of a collective defensive pressure that asphyxiates opponents in
their lungs, their muscles, and their brains. The goal is to induce
fatigue and poor decisions, so that they concede possession as
quickly as possible—and preferably in vulnerable positions on
the field. One hallmark of collective pressure in modern soccer
is the high defensive line that teams establish to push possession
upfield and stay compact with the rest of the team as it tries to
force turnovers. "The idea of high pressure is to make sure they
can't have the time to think and play that pass," Kompany says.
"In their brains it suffocates"—that word again—"because they
have to defend as well. It costs them a lot of energy. So what you
want to do is make sure that by the time they get the ball, they
don't have the time, the energy, or the power to get themselves
out and hurt you. *That* is what you are doing, actually."

Pressure *has* to be collective, however, for it to work. If one
player, even a forward, is lazy and refuses to take part, the entire operation is rendered ineffective. Pressure is only as good as
its weakest link. "Anybody who has been defending will know
that it can only be easy when the pressure is intense all over the
pitch," Kompany says. "And then you pick up a lot of balls, and
it looks easy, but it's not. Any amount of space, any line that
gets broken—that's an unusual amount of space to cover and
you lose the advantage. Usually teams play a high line because
the benefits outweigh the risks. But everyone knows the risks. If
you have a fast striker, he can damage you. If people are out of

[defensive] position and they can't get back in time physically, it weakens you."

The most aggressive teams deploy pressure over nearly the entire field. But other outfits have different defensive strategies. For Kompany the conscious decisions on which parts of the field to engage in defensively and which parts to concede are intriguing ones. "There are many ways of defending," he says. "If you play for a team like Barcelona and the whole team is putting pressure on the opponents, then you have got to put pressure on straight away. But if you play in a more Italian type of way, you kind of have to take in the pressure and let the [other team] have a little bit of control—and only make sure you press in the zones that are yours."

The conventional wisdom among soccer cognoscenti is that the sport has fewer world-class central defenders than it did two decades ago. Paolo Maldini, the great defender for AC Milan and Italy, glumly nodded his head when I asked him about it not long ago. "The game has changed," Maldini told me. "Central defenders—they play the ball more now. Twenty years ago they were only defenders, and only a few of them were confident with the ball. But they're also losing the ability to mark one against one, to mark on corners. The art of defending is losing some characteristics from the '80s. It really bothers me, especially at the top levels—Champions League and national teams. The game has changed a lot, but I still think having a great defense makes you, long term, a better team. And a winning team, too." If you ask Maldini to name his favorite centerbacks today, the first name he mentions is Real Madrid's Sergio Ramos. "But sometimes," Maldini adds, "he forgets about defending."

Kompany agrees with Maldini and thinks he knows why.

"Even from 10 years ago," he says, "being a good defender has changed completely. You used to be able to sit back, see the game, and just deal with your man. Usually you had support from all over the pitch. Every defender's dream is to play in a team like the great Milan [of the late 1980s and early 1990s] with [Franco] Baresi and Maldini, with a philosophy that was ideal for defensive players." That credo, put simply, was that defenders focused on defending. "But football has evolved. It's more dynamic. There's more change of position. Fullbacks go all the way [upfield] and turn into wingers. Strikers are quicker, they aren't naive, and so many players can put in a last pass. To be comfortable in all those new things is a very difficult task."

As someone who's immersed completely in the sport of soccer, Kompany loves watching the game on television. From a pure defending perspective, he says he's looking for specific things from centerbacks when he's studying them on the screen. "I want to feel the player is in control all the time, that a mistake doesn't cause a panic reaction," he explains. "I want to see that the defender has seen something—a run that wasn't necessarily his man—and he has been able to adapt his position. And I want to know that the defender is kind of in and out. Don't stay stuck to a striker and just follow him around. Be in and out, and then you just decide who has got to be where and compensate if something is needed." *In and out* is one of Kompany's mantras; he says it more often than a California fast-food connoisseur. But his point is clear: The best centerbacks have a holistic view of defending.

What's more, today's centerbacks are expected to be more skillful on the ball. With the increasing use of a high defensive line, they need to start the attack from a more advanced position than ever. At the same time, forwards are pressing them more tightly in an effort to win the ball in a dangerous position. For Kompany, modern soccer requires that you study not just the attacking tendencies of opposing forwards but those forwards' *defensive* proclivities as well. Take Luis Suárez of Barcelona and Uruguay, one of the most lethal centerforwards today. To Kompany, Suárez is like one of Pamplona's running bulls: a threat who's not just powerful but devious and clever as well. "When you're on the ball and facing your own goal, he's always looking for your blind side, and it's really difficult to turn, not knowing where he is," says Kompany. "He's an aggressive striker who's going to try to nick the ball off you. [Carlos] Tévez is also an aggressive striker. With other strikers you can actually try something [offensively] because they just *pretend* to press you. If you know your strikers, it just limits the amount of mistakes."

Kompany's respect for Suárez is mutual. I interviewed Suárez in early 2014, when he was playing for Liverpool, and asked him who was the toughest defender he had ever faced. His answer: Kompany. Watching video of Suárez and Kompany battling each other during Premier League games between Liverpool and Manchester City, I couldn't help but imagine them as a real-life version of the wolf and the sheepdog in the old Looney Tunes cartoons ("Mornin', Sam." "Mornin', Ralph."), who would inflict mayhem on each other, only to punch their time cards and exchange pleasantries at the end of the workday as they headed home with their lunch pails.

"Playing against Suárez has always been an interesting battle for me," says Kompany, who continued to face the Uruguayan in the Champions League after Suárez moved to Barcelona. "I've loved many of them, and I've suffered in some of them as well.

Players like Suárez take it as far as they can. Of course, he's technically gifted, and he's got a nose for goals, and he's got strength, which people don't often know about. But he'll play on the edge every single game, and he'll try to catch you off guard. You can literally see in his eyes that he's looking for you to lose a moment of attention to make use of that. He's always got movements and countermovements in the box, and then it's just that winner's mentality, knowing that he wants to get on the end of a cross or a pass."

Yet Suárez is only one of the many types of forwards that Kompany has encountered. "You've got other challenges, like Zlatan Ibrahimović and people who are pure strength and experience and cleverness," Kompany says. "I would always say the hardest strikers to play against are those who are just desperate to score. All the others, they can cause for a nice YouTube video, but ultimately you can handle it. The hardest ones to play against are those who sometimes don't even appear to be dominant, but they are always, always so hungry and desperate to score."

From a preparation perspective, Kompany spends time before each game viewing scouting material on a team and individual basis. It's naive to go into any game, he says, without being aware of an opponent's strengths and trying to take advantage of the team's weaknesses. "And on a personal level, I like to see some images from the players I'm going to play against, like a driver who's going to scout the track before he gets on it," Kompany adds. "Everybody has a pattern, and the best strikers are extremely good at certain things. It's good to be completely aware of what they do, so you're always a step ahead. The rest is just trust. I will only doubt myself if I haven't prepared well, but if I haven't prepared well then that's a professional mistake, so that won't happen. So I prepare well, and then I say to myself, 'I've done it before, so I'll do it again.' That's it."

Man City's coaching staff will usually prepare a 15-minute series of video clips for Kompany to study the forwards he'll be coming up against in the next game. It helps, obviously, that he is a Premier League veteran who has catalogued his own experiences against certain players over the years. "The game is evolving massively on the video analysis side, so we've got virtually everything at our disposal," Kompany says in City's state-of-the-art video theater. "I'll watch the 15-minute clip about the opposition, and I'll focus on what those players are used to doing. You already know, for example, that Peter Crouch likes going back post so he can flick it back for a smaller striker who comes in and creates the danger. He used to do that with Jermain Defoe. I'm not saying you can always handle it, but if you know it, you have an advantage."

One of our conversations takes place the day after a City game against crosstown rival Manchester United. Kompany went 90 minutes not long after returning from injury and helped limit the influence of United attackers Marcus Rashford and Anthony Martial in a 0–0 tie at the Etihad. (Ibrahimović was out injured.) "They are the most difficult players to play against, when you have a high line against extremely fast strikers," Kompany says. "Martial and Rashford are definitely in that category. You really have to be careful, because from the moment you are exposed, they're going all the way, and that can hurt. No one has enough pace to catch someone like Rashford when he has a head start on you, so it's all about anticipating what could happen. You know that he's looking to make a run in your back. So with a little bit of experience, what you do is you either physically block him, so he can't even turn, or you make sure you have enough support before you intervene. Everything's a challenge, right?"

As I listen to Kompany, I'm struck by some of the language he uses to talk about his job as a defender. Some of it sounds like the phrasing used by Javier Hernández and Christian Pulisic to describe their jobs as *attackers*. Anticipation, after all, is one of Chicharito's keys to his movement to beat defenders in the box. And when Pulisic says one of his biggest challenges is when a defender gets "in your back," it doesn't sound much different than Kompany being concerned about Rashford getting "in your back." Granted, Pulisic is describing an opponent literally bumping up against his back (the body part), while Kompany is referring to his "back" as the giant space between him and the goal. But the similarities in language are uncanny and suggest that the push-pull between attackers and defenders maybe isn't all that different after all.

Had Ibrahimović been available for their game the night before, Kompany would have prepared in a completely different way. But the Belgian's speed, size, and strength—to say nothing of his positioning—mean he's equipped to take on just about any kind of forward. "If you play against Zlatan, you know that he will make something happen," Kompany says. "And you have to be extremely careful because he can seem like he's not in the game, but then he's the one who scores. When you play against someone like Rashford, you know that he's extremely confident. He'll attack you and keep attacking you, and he won't be fazed by anything. So they're different challenges, but I do believe that, with preparation, you can be a match."

To succeed as a defender, he argues, you have to possess two qualities: the knowledge of how to defend correctly, and the technical and physical abilities to execute that knowledge on the field. Many defenders, he says, have one but not the other. "I know exactly *how* to do it," he says, "but in a game of 90 minutes, when you're tired and you've played your third game of the week? Mistakes happen. I know I *know* the right things—but executing them? Eighty percent of the time."

He lets out a belly laugh. "It depends on the striker you're marking, too."

THE BEST ADVICE THAT KOMPANY ever received was also the worst advice. When he was a youth player in Belgium, he says, one of his coaches told him, "You're a big defender. Stick to what you're good at." In essence, that coach—Kompany says he was one of the exceptions at his club, Anderlecht—didn't expect him to become technically gifted on the ball. "And that just *did* it for me," says Kompany, snapping his fingers. "[I wanted] people to be surprised to see my skills, that I could do things that a striker does. I was obsessed by it, and I kept working until they said, 'Vince is really good when he plays from the back!' They used the words *elegant* and *flair*. I was never as good as some of the most gifted players, but I was better than anyone in my position for a long time."

The youth system at Anderlecht was modeled on the famed Ajax academy in the Netherlands. The emphasis was on producing ball-playing defenders, and Kompany's obsession with passing and technical skills paid off. The ball stayed on the ground. Kompany's youth teams almost never played in the air. "We weren't allowed to kick the ball all the way upfield, so you kind of evolved into the player you needed to be. You took a lot of risk, but that's what they asked for," he says. "I was always a defender and defensive midfielder. The way we grew up at Anderlecht, it was interchangeable in the sense that the defender was asked to break the lines with the ball. And in that case, the defensive midfielder would become the defender. Everything was based around being a ball-playing defender." When you watch video with Kompany and he wins a ball in the defensive half before launching into a 60-yard run downfield with it, the temptation is to compare him to Franz Beckenbauer, the legendary German defender. But Kompany often smiles and calls it "going Anderlecht."

Kompany grew up modeling his game on other graceful defenders and defensive midfielders with good ball skills. "I used to be a big fan of Marcel Desailly," Kompany says. "He played as a defensive midfielder at Milan and Marseille, and then he moved back to central defender. At Chelsea and his national team he was always between two positions, so there are a lot of similarities. I was also a great admirer of Patrick Vieira. But I never really identified myself to another player because I was cheeky in my head, thinking I needed to be better. But I liked the all-around presence that they had on the pitch."

In some ways, Anderlecht's insistence on its youth teams keeping the ball on the ground is similar—in effect, if not in intention—to the rules adopted by U.S. Soccer in 2015 that eliminate heading the ball by children age 10 and younger and limit the amount of heading in practice from the ages of 11 to 13. Although U.S. Soccer cited a desire to prevent head injuries in young players, a number of former U.S. senior national team players criticized the rule, arguing that youngsters wouldn't be able to learn the correct technique of heading. Yet Kompany's own experience suggests otherwise. "It's funny. One of the strongest parts of my game today is heading," Kompany says, "and that only really developed when I started playing at the professional level. In the youth teams all we did was passing."

The ability to deliver the right pass—whether it's short to the side, a diagonal arrow upfield on a dime, or something in-between—is a fundamental skill for the modern centerback. Man City has put together clips and divided them into four categories: Distribution, Aerial Duels, Proactive Defending, and Goals. In the Distribution footage Kompany regularly completes lengthy passes with just the right weight, direction, and distance—the kind that would make NFL quarterback Aaron Rodgers proud. "The biggest pass for a defender is a pass forward," Kompany says, as the video shows him unspooling a ball from the back, over the midfield, to forward Wilfried Bony. "If you break a line, you can actually take out three or four players at a time. But you have to be really careful. If I'm a defender, that's the ball I'm trying to intercept. You have to know when to pick your pass. When I was younger, I would just try to [make long passes] all the time. Now I'll [mix in] a side pass every now and then."

In the Proactive Defending section, Kompany repeatedly steps in to intercept passes with an anticipation that borders on eerie. He almost never struggles with his man picking off the ball—the word he likes to use here is *tidy*. On defending an opposing striker, he says, "Anticipate. Read his body language. Know your opponent, because marking someone is actually just guessing where he's going. You don't want to be always following what he does. One of the things I've realized with experience is that things come more easily. Most things you've seen already. When a *quick* striker [comes back to the ball], you know he actually wants to go long. When a *big* striker comes short, he wants to hold the ball and bring someone else into play. You don't want to be stuck to that guy because he'll turn you. What he doesn't want is that little bit of space where he can't feel you but you can still"—here he claps—*"get in and out."*

What becomes clear is that defending is rarely about a single player. *Is there pressure on the ball? Is your centerback partner close enough? Does he know you're providing cover for him? Is your back line connected and moving together?* "With defending, people overestimate the importance of actually being good [individually]," says Kompany. "The most important thing is to be a good defensive unit. I'm 60 percent better if the guys next to me have an understanding."

The deployment of those defenders also comes into play. As Kompany notes, Belgium took a conservative approach under its Euro 2016 coach, Marc Wilmots, using traditional centerbacks at the fullback positions and rarely asking them to join the attack. Under Wilmots's replacement, Roberto Martínez, Belgium is using its surfeit of centerbacks to play a three-man back line with true wingers. As for Man City, Pellegrini played with four in the back and asked his fullbacks to maraud forward constantly, often leaving defenders in one-on-one situations when the counter came back their way. Under Guardiola, Kompany explains, City still plays a high defensive line, but there is greater positional balance in the team.

"There's a big difference," he says. "Under Pellegrini, we had two fullbacks that would go all the way, two wingers that came inside to play in a number 10 role—both of them—and ultimately we had three number 10s and one striker. And of the two defensive midfielders, one of them was Yaya Touré, who was still an offensive player, so we had a maximum three players concerned with defending. Whereas [under Guardiola] we have more balance in that sense. We have five players who will try to control things and still participate in the game. Teams find it difficult to counterattack because we are in the right positions. We played a very high line [under Pellegrini] as well, but we committed even more people forward."

As a centerback Kompany tends to stay at home, but there are occasions when he moves up in front of the opposing goal. That's not usually during the run of play. "The thing at City is that there's so much quality up front, you would just get in the way," Kompany says. Once in a blue moon, though, if City is truly desperate, he'll become another forward in the box, as he did on the famous stoppage-time goal by Sergio (Kun) Agüero in 2012 that clinched the Premier League title for City on the final day of the season. "I believe to this day that my dummy run made the space for Kun," Kompany jokes. (Look at the video; he's not *wrong*.) More commonly, though, Kompany creeps up into the opponent's box just for the scoring opportunities presented by corners and free kicks. What's he thinking as he does that? "I've found out that the times I don't believe I'm going to score, I never score," he says. "So I always need to feel like I'm going to score. You might get four or five goals a season that way, but if you don't think you're going to score, then just don't go. That's what I've learned. And I have had many days like this where I was thinking, *I'm tired. I'm probably not going to connect with the ball.*"

On the video screen, in a Premier League clip from 2013, Kompany is being marked on a corner kick by notorious Liverpool shirt-puller Martin Škrtel. The scene is soccer's answer to Greco-Roman wrestling. "I usually have the biggest guy from the other team hanging on my shoulders," Kompany says of the 6-foot-3 Slovakian. Stationed 10 yards from the goal, Kompany plants his right elbow on the chest of Škrtel, whose left hand is grabbing so much of Kompany's jersey that half of the Belgian's back is exposed. They dance together in an awkward minuet toward the edge of the 6-yard box, where Kompany ultimately beats Škrtel to the spot and—just as Kompany described—barely needs to jump before nodding David Silva's corner kick into the net. The recoil puts Kompany on his back, but he leaps up to celebrate with his teammates. Kompany says Škrtel, who now plays in Turkey, is hardly the only excessive grappler he has encountered in England. In fact, he adds, the Premier League "has a lot less than other leagues. If you play against Italian teams, you feel like the rules have been changed, like they do anything they want. In England it's usually a fair battle."

Kompany's goals for club and country have allowed him, on occasion, to pop up in TV highlights in a positive way, but largely the task of defending is a thankless one. Centerbacks typically draw attention only when things go wrong. "The hardest part is just the unpredictable stuff," Kompany says. "You can do everything right, but then you'll have a ricochet, or an own goal, or someone not following his man, or you get an overload on the flanks and a cross comes in and there's nothing you can do. But then you're the guy picking the ball out of the net with the goalkeeper. You're the guy being blamed for something. And if you really know football, you know there is a bit more to that action."

Kompany smiles. "If someone just watches the highlights, they probably won't have a lot of respect for defenders," he says. "But if they watch the whole game, they will respect what you do."

It's a shame, really, that we don't see more defensive highlights on television shows, not least because the defensive side of soccer is just as important as its attacking aspects. There's beauty in great defending, and few practitioners are more elegant at the job than Vincent Kompany.

SOMETIMES, THE BEST DEFENSE AGAINST a superstar like Lionel Messi is to prevent him from receiving the ball in the first place. In one of Manchester City's Champions League games against Barcelona, defender Gerard Piqué fires a 25-yard pass on the ground toward Messi. This time Kompany has support behind him, so he can take a risk. Kompany gets an early jump, having read the pass, and his feet move with a combination of lightness and speed that is reminiscent of a ballet dancer. He doesn't need to clatter into Messi, nor does he even touch the Argentine. Kompany simply reaches the ball first and is already looking up to make a pass upfield in the other direction to start the counterattack. "It's all about how much cover you have, and then you can go," Kompany says. "Communication is really important. Maybe someone gave me the shout: '*You can go, Vinnie!*'"

What's so difficult about facing Messi is his relentlessness. He's coming at you the entire game, and even if you slow him down him a few times, all he needs is one opening and he'll bury you. (Barcelona will end up winning this game 2–0, with Messi scoring from the penalty spot and Kompany's centerback partner Martín Demichelis being sent off.) While stopping Messi in a one-on-one battle is a point of pride, Kompany knows that you can't hope to defend Messi individually over a 90-minute game. "When you come to players like Messi, it's always about a team effort," Kompany says. "I don't think anyone's got a solution as to how to stop him, but he'd probably admit himself that, when he gets really crowded, it becomes a little more difficult. The very best attackers I've ever played against, they've always got that split second faster, where even if you know where they're going or where they're going to shoot, they're just that little bit faster to take the shot where you can't really do anything about it. So sometimes it's not even about doing the right or the wrong thing. It's just he'll do it that fast, and you hope it'll go your way. It's always a team effort. But individually, if he's one-on-one and he's got the goal in his sight? If he's 40 meters away, maybe you have a chance. If he's closer, then you really need to be at your best to stop him getting a shot off."

Different attackers represent different challenges, however. In another scene, from a game against Arsenal, the Gunners have possession near the center circle. Stationed 30 yards from his goal, Kompany is in his usual right centerback position. Arsenal's Olivier Giroud, a sturdy striker who plays as a target forward, moves toward Kompany and tries to post him up like a center in a basketball game who's asking for the pass. "Giroud is a big striker," Kompany says. "He was looking for me. If you feel that he's got you pinned down, it's finished. *Get out of it.*" Before Giroud can park his butt on Kompany, the Belgian sidesteps to his right and tiptoes around Giroud in time to intercept the pass. "I had momentum and I could just nick it," says Kompany. "You have to look at the pace of the striker sometimes. You can make up ground on him. You cannot make up ground on Suárez, for example. But Giroud is stronger to hold the ball, so every striker's got his own qualities." Yet Kompany isn't done on the screen. After winning the ball in his own defensive third of the field, he goes Anderlecht on Arsenal, launching himself into a 70-yard dribbling run in which he beats five men and ends up near the left corner flag. It's a jaw-dropping play—how many other centerbacks in the world would even try it, especially when their team is down a man?—but Kompany isn't an ordinary defender. "You try to go as far as you can," he says. Finally, his attempted cross is intercepted. Kompany groans. "Wrong decision on my part, especially because we were with 10 men."

As attackers go, Diego Costa is more mobile than Giroud and more physical than Messi. Those qualities are on display in another video clip from a game against Chelsea. With Chelsea attacking down its left side and City's right fullback pushed forward, Costa drags Kompany out wide and receives a pass near the touchline 40 yards from goal. Kompany has defensive cover behind him, but he has to defend Costa one-on-one. With his back to the goal, Costa has a terrific first touch, flipping the ball into space down the line, turning, and running onto it again. It looks like he has beaten Kompany, who's trailing the play. But not so fast. Kompany closes the gap in an instant, using his quick feet, and Costa has to strain for his second touch, which turns the ball inside toward the goal. Costa is nothing if not dogged, but Kompany employs his arms and his trunk to ride Costa out of the way and latch onto the ball just on the edge of the penalty box. Kompany turns to dribble out of danger, and now Costa pursues him like an angry Rottweiler, at least until the referee whistles a foul on the Chelsea striker. The City fans are standing and roaring. To mix it up and win against Costa, one of the Premier League's archvillains, is a badge of honor. "If you go out of position, you need to take something," Kompany says. "And that is actually a good move from Costa, but on that occasion I was stronger."

The tactical bromide in soccer is that you should have one more centerback—a spare man—than the other team has center-forwards. That way there is protection. Cover. But Kompany says he thrives on one-on-one situations. "If I'm one-versus-one, I like it," he explains. "As long as I have to deal with just one man. Problem for us—in my case, anyway—is when I have to deal with two or three. But one man is not a problem."

The above are all nominally one-on-one events, though not entirely. On the Giroud and Costa plays, Kompany knows he has cover behind him in case something goes wrong. The lesson is important: Defending doesn't happen in a vacuum. In another clip against Manchester United, an unpressured Michael Carrick sends a pass to Danny Welbeck, who has made a diagonal run from left to right across City's penalty box. Kompany, the right centerback, stays with Welbeck as he crosses the box, while Demichelis (the left centerback) moves into the space Kompany has vacated to cover for him. Seeing his partner, Kompany knows he can go in on Welbeck, steal the ball, and end the threat. "This is probably the most important thing in defending," Kompany says. "It's all about covering. For me to be tight [on Welbeck], I need to know [Demichelis] has got my back. So I come across, Martín is coming back in, and then I finish the deal and try to play it out as tidy as you can."

The key phrase here is *play it out*. Kompany almost never just boots the ball downfield after winning it in his own end. Even when he's in danger of losing it in an awful place to do so, he takes the risk to find a teammate and keep possession. Finally, I ask him: Do you *always* play the ball out of the back? "It depends on the team," he says. "Some managers tell you that you have to, and then you just do it. You find a way. But usually the team also moves straight away. You can play out of the back if everyone is moving around to receive the ball. But if the team is expecting you to clear it, just clear it." Once again: No decision takes place in a one-on-one vacuum.

I have other questions, too. Important ones. Like, *How do you know when it's a good time to step up on the back line?* His answer makes me think back to Chicharito's line about smelling the anticipation in the box. "I think a little bit of intuition comes into it," Kompany says. "You always have to make sure you have the advantage on the striker. I like to step up when I know the striker is backpedaling a little bit, because then you have double the force. The best moment to step up is when the striker is backing off and he has his back to the goal. Be careful of stepping up when the striker is just pretending to go short and then he goes long. Those are things you learn. If there's no pressure on the ball, you can't step up or you have to be really careful."

Another type of hairy defensive moment appears on the screen: a cutback pass from deep in the corner into the box. In a game against West Brom, Billy Jones dribbles the ball wide down the right side. City's back line has continued sliding down closer and closer to its goal, leaving space at the top of the box for forward Stéphane Sessègnon. Jones cuts his pass on the ground back to Sessègnon, who's just 12 yards out from the goal. On the edge of the 6-yard box between Sessègnon and goalkeeper Joe Hart, Kompany has limited options. "Cutbacks are the hardest balls to deal with," Kompany says. "The striker has got such a big advantage. I can throw my body at it, but you could easily have an own goal here." In this situation, Kompany decides to go horizontal, making himself as wide as possible, and turn his left shoulder toward the ground in a barrel roll to avoid drawing a hand-ball penalty. Sessègnon's one-time shot thumps Kompany in the back of his right leg and deflects just over Hart's crossbar, barely avoiding an own goal. Watching the replay, Kompany breathes an audible sigh of relief. "Judgment call," he says. He knows how close it came to being a disaster.

Kompany says the best defenders—the most instinctual ones, at least—are the ones who can prevent goals when the team defense is in shambles "and you can make something look good that was actually a horrendous situation." In another video clip, Chelsea's Cesc Fàbregas is 30 yards from goal and, despite having seven City defenders in the area, completely unpressured on the ball. Fàbregas sees Diego Costa making a run behind Kompany toward goal in the box. "This is not ideal," says an exasperated Kompany. "There's nobody on him. We have seven players and there is no pressure and there is a massive gap [between Kompany and centerback partner Eliaquim Mangala]. At this moment I would have been shouting to Mangala to come closer because the ball is shifting the other way." Mangala takes one step toward Kompany, who ends up saving the day by rushing over to pick off Fàbregas's pass to Costa. In the end, Kompany makes a horrendous situation look good. He does this often enough that it is not a coincidence.

Kompany's individual value to Manchester City is irrefutable, not least when you examine the data. Using Opta's statistical database, analyst Ben Torvaney sought to compare Man City's defensive performance when Kompany has been on the field to when he has not. As Torvaney notes, there is often reason to be skeptical of "with-or-without-you" statistics in soccer, since soccer is a complex sport played by 22 people at a time. But large sample sizes can alleviate concerns, and Kompany provides a large sample size, since he has played for City since 2008—and, unfortunately, because he has also missed a lot of games due to injury during that time.

To examine the effect Kompany has had on team performance, Torvaney analyzed Manchester City's Premier League and Champions League games from the start of 2013–14 until the end of the 2016–17 season and divided them into two groups: games in which Kompany did not play and games in which Kompany played at least 60 minutes. He then looked at the performance of the Man City team in each of these groups for a selection of metrics: the number of successful passes in the final third the opponent makes per game; the number of crosses conceded per game (excluding corners); the number of shots conceded per game; and the proportion of shots conceded from within the penalty box per game.

	GAMES	FINAL-THIRD PASSES	OPP GOALS	% SHOTS IN BOX	OPP CROSSES	TOTAL SHOTS AGAINST
DID NOT PLAY	77	67.4	1.3	61.8	11.3	10.3
PLAYED > 60	85	77.1	1.0	52.1	12.5	9.5

With Kompany in the team, the number of goals and shots conceded is lower. It's possible also to dig a bit deeper and try to find statistical fingerprints for *how* he improves the defense. As Torvaney notes, one of the first places to look is the proportion of shots taken inside the penalty box. Without Kompany, about 62 percent of the team's shots conceded take place from inside the box. But in games where Kompany has played at least 60 minutes, this figure drops to 52 percent. That tells us that not only does the number of chances conceded decrease with Kompany in the team, but the *quality* of those chances is reduced as well. Teams find it harder to create shooting opportunities in dangerous areas.

We can learn even more by looking at the opponents' final-third pass volume and the crosses conceded. Unlike in the case of shots conceded, both of these metrics are higher when Kompany has been in the team. Without Kompany in the team, Man City's opponents have taken more shots of a higher average quality, and they have taken fewer passes to do it. This suggests to Torvaney that with Kompany on the field, teams have found it harder to progress upfield, ending up with more sterile possession in the final third. The fact that more crosses are conceded in games with Kompany is consistent with this view; teams had more difficulty attacking through the center of the field and were forced to go wide more frequently. These kinds of chances tend to be easier to defend (especially if you have Kompany to defend them). Another point to note is that, as a possession team, Man City is vulnerable to fast, direct counterattacks. The data we see here is also consistent with City dealing with these kinds of attacks more effectively with Kompany on the field.

Still, outstanding individual performances do not make for one of the best defensive units in European soccer, Kompany believes. In the same way that Chicharito Hernández and the Mexican national team have systematized patterns for their attack, Kompany wants Man City to have what he calls "systematic behavior" at all times from a defensive perspective. It's not overly complicated, he says. The elite teams work together, reading the scene, rotating, and covering for each other defensively. "That's the big difference," Kompany says, "not just between [individual] defenders, but between the best teams in the world and the rest. If you have this systematic behavior all over the pitch for 90 minutes, you can become a team that looks invincible."

If Kompany plays in World Cup 2018 with Belgium, it is almost certain that manager Roberto Martínez will use Kompany in a three-man back line (with three centerbacks), instead of deploying four defenders in the back (with two centerbacks and two fullbacks). I tell Kompany in April 2017 that I assume that change from Manchester City's four-man back line will be a significant adjustment for him. But he says I assume wrongly.

"You can start in a formation, and during the game it evolves so much," he explains. "I'll give the example of yesterday's [Man City] match. The buildup that we had [with four in the back] wasn't so different than the buildup with three in the back. If you think of it, either [of central midfielders] Yaya [Touré] or Fernandinho was dropping, therefore we're always building up with three centrally, and two wide players would push up or fill places in midfield, but still with our wingers playing like wing-backs. I think a tactically mature team needs to be able to adjust, especially in possession, to the demands of the game. And then, defensively, I think it really becomes a back three or a back five when you defend really low. Otherwise, it's still the same principle: You've got a certain number of people that need to control the counterattacks and a certain number of people that need to make it happen for goals. Where they are in relation to each other will roughly be the same whether you're playing in a 4-3-3 or a 4-4-2 or a 3-5-2. It's only details that change."

No matter how Belgium lines up, there is no denying that it has one of its most talented soccer generations in history. The Red Devils failed to qualify for a major tournament between the 2002 and the 2014 World Cups, and yet the skill on the team is so deep these days—Belgium's top 20 players would be among the world's top three national teams in terms of open-market value—that quarterfinal runs at World Cup 2014 and Euro 2016 were considered disappointments. How stacked is Belgium? Well, its ranks include a Who's Who of elite European club soccer, from forwards (Romelu Lukaku, Michy Batshuayi, Yannick Carrasco, Divock Origi, Christian Benteke) to wingers (Eden Hazard, Dries Mertens) to central midfielders (Kevin De Bruyne, Axel Witsel, Radja Nainggolan, Marouane Fellaini) to defenders (Kompany, Jan Vertonghen, Toby Alderweireld) to goalkeepers (Thibaut Courtois).

Some national teams are typically better than the sum of their parts, at least if you consider the level of the clubs represented by the players. Other national teams are typically less than the sum of their parts. Belgium, unfortunately, has drawn this reputation, and losing to Wales in the Euro 2016 quarterfinals didn't help matters. Kompany knows what it takes to win trophies with Man City, obviously, and he doesn't see any reason why Belgium's reputation should be set in stone. "Our national team is not a winning national team yet, to be quite simple," he says. "So all of us have a duty to present ourselves with the hunger of people that still have everything to win." Kompany thinks back to Euro 2016, when he was unable to play due to injury, and remembers hammering Italy 3–1 in a friendly a few months before the tournament. But when the games started for real in France, it was Italy that "upset" Belgium 2–0. That defeat stuck with Kompany. "You only really find out about a team when you enter a big tournament," he says. "It's good to be aware of signs of overconfidence, but the main thing is to be hungry like no other team to achieve something that is, for all of us, unique in our careers and our lives."

One of Belgium's most important tools, of course, is Kompany. It was a measure of his value to the team that, as soon as he started playing again for Man City at the end of the 2016–17 season, Kompany became a starter again for Belgium in his first opportunity to play for the national team in months after his injuries. As Martínez put it when I asked him about Kompany: "There are players that know what you have to do to win games in certain moments, and it goes away from individual talent. It goes into becoming a team. Vincent has got the know-how and the experience. He will be very, very important for us."

Ultimately, the most significant lesson I take away from my time with Kompany may be this: Even though he's one of the top centerbacks in the world, he stands out even more because he combines that talent with a rare degree of leadership and an awareness that the individual is always part of a larger team. When Kompany says, "I'm 60 percent better if the guys next to me have an understanding," he believes that with his heart and soul.

At the same time, Kompany accepts that the future of the sport will involve even more refinement of what makes players different from one another, and he's just fine with that. "The game is moving toward a high specification of the positions," he says. "We used to train and develop on kind of a general football idea. But now players develop on a position idea very early. From the ages of 8 and 10, you already see there are fullbacks and wingers and central defenders with specific training sessions. They'll watch everything at the top level and be prepared for this, not just when they get here but 10 years before that. They won't be just asking of a central defender to be big and heading the ball, but they'll demand they be good technically, to be quick and mobile as well, to handle strikers who can do that. It will be more toward what American sport already does: specialization. That adaptation of training sessions and working schedules toward games to get them even better in their positions."

If Kompany sounds like someone who plans to stay in the sport after he's done playing, that would be an accurate assessment. "After spending so many years in football and thinking so many years about football, it's a logical step for me to stay in the game and give something back or offer my knowledge and experience to more people," he says one day. "I'd like to see if maybe my vision is what people want to follow as well. I'm pretty sure I'll stay in football."

That may disappoint the people who want Kompany to become a politician. But he's a football man, after all.

4

THE GOALKEEPER

Manuel Neuer's Risky Security

AT THE HIGHEST LEVEL, MODERN SOCCER HAS A LOT IN COM-mon with the German autobahn. The speed of the game has no limits these days—every second counts—and the players are like finely calibrated sports cars: faster, sleeker, and more powerful than ever. Soccer's movement, its attacking and defensive pressure, is constant. And yet there remains an order to things, a reminder that even life on the edge has forces that prevent chaos. No player straddles those worlds better than Manuel Neuer, the planet's premier goalkeeper, who has redefined his position in a way that hasn't been done for decades. "I'm a little bit risky, but I'm standing for security and protection, and you have to give your teammates that feeling as well," says Neuer, the captain for World Cup champion Germany and Bayern Munich. "In life, I'm a guy who likes to drive a car quite fast, but I wear a seat belt at the same time."

Surrounded by Champions League trophies in the Bayern Munich boardroom, the 6-foot-4, 210-pound Neuer, with piercing blue eyes, a square jaw, and beige-blond hair, has folded his sturdy frame into a leather office chair. He likes to say hello with an athletic handshake—fingers up, not out, connecting mostly with the thumbs—and the literal wink of an eye, a suggestion of confidence mixed with a hint of mischief. More than any other figure in this book, Neuer in person gives off an aura of physical *power*, a combination of size, strength, and the potential of movement at a high speed. If he set his mind to it, you think, he could probably put on enough weight to be a linebacker for an American football team.

Like most Germans, Neuer speaks better English than he lets on at first, and he draws a special pleasure from discussing his ultimate fast-lane experience: Germany's Round of 16 victory against Algeria in World Cup 2014. To watch Neuer's highlight video from the game, which includes an astonishing 5 clearances and 20 touches *outside* his penalty box, is to see a goalkeeper pushing the outer limits of what's physically possible and, perhaps, mentally sane.

Time and again, with Germany's attack-minded high back line pushed up near midfield, Algeria sends passes through and over the back four, hoping fleet forwards Islam Slimani and Sofiane Feghouli can run onto the ball for a lightning-strike goal in the rain of Porto Alegre, Brazil. But there's no joy for the men in green, no *alegría* for Algeria. There's Neuer launching himself 35 yards from his goal, racing Slimani stride for stride into the corner and sliding to block his cross before it can reach the penalty area. There's Neuer hurtling outside his box again and propelling his head at a dangerous diagonal ball before crashing into the onrushing Slimani. And there's Neuer covering on a misplayed back pass, accelerating like a dragster and clearing the ball from danger an instant before Aissa Mandi's arrival.

For anyone watching the game on television, the sight of a goalkeeper in a different-colored uniform charging out into uncustomary parts of the field might have given the impression that a well-conditioned pitch invader had rushed onto the field. But, no, it was just Neuer. He may look like a madman at first, but his objective is clear: to prevent as many scoring chances as possible *before* they materialize, even if that means taking sphincter-tightening risks as the last line of defense. "It's up to me to help my defenders," he says, "and it's better for me to get the ball before the striker than to [wait and] have a one-on-one situation in the box. That's more dangerous than to go out, because the striker has the chance to score a goal. If he can't get the ball, he won't get *any* opportunity."

The downside of Neuer's approach is the soccer version of hara-kiri. If he misjudges the speed and trajectory of the ball or the striker and arrives too late, he may concede a goal and look silly in the process. "I don't feel the fear in my head in this moment," he says. "I am always thinking positive. It's all about the first step. If I think I will get the ball, I go out. I can't stop halfway because the goal is empty and the player would have the opportunity to shoot on goal. You make the reaction, and then, of course, you have to be sure to get the ball. But it's years of practice. You can't say from one day to the other: 'Now I will do it,' you know? You have to *feel* it."

The Algeria game also featured special circumstances that created an extreme situation. Germany deployed relatively slow centerbacks (Per Mertesacker and Shkodran Mustafi), Algeria's front-line speed was formidable, and, Neuer says, he could station himself higher up the field due to the ball skidding faster on the wet sod. What's more, he thinks his early stops put a degree of fear into the opposing strikers, causing them to pull out early. "I noticed a lot of the players didn't want to go into the one-on-one because I'm big," he says. You can almost hear the groans from forwards, who tend to believe (rightly) that goalkeepers are given more latitude than defenders to initiate contact in the box without fearing a penalty and with the benefit of being able to use their hands high in the air to clear the ball.

Neuer's "heat map" for the Algeria game, which shows the location of his touches and positioning, is unlike anything you would associate with a traditional goalkeeper. It's as though he's playing two positions instead of one. In fact, Neuer has taken coloring outside the lines (of his penalty box) to such an extent that he's already considered by many observers as one of the sport's greatest goalkeeping innovators. In 2014 Neuer was World Cup champion Germany's only finalist for the FIFA Ballon d'Or—the world player of the year—alongside Cristiano Ronaldo and Lionel Messi. In a stunning upset, the German language has yet to yield an 18-letter word for the goalkeeper position as played by Neuer. Give the Germans some time. For now, though, English has spawned a 16-letter handle for Neuer that will be hard to top, one that produces a wide smile from the big German.

The sweeper keeper.

·

AS A POSITION ON THE soccer field, the sweeper—or at least the sweeper of the 20th century—is an anachronism, a relic from a bygone era. Stationed centrally behind the back line, the sweeper (also sometimes called a *libero*) cleaned up the defenders' mistakes and had the freedom to roam like a safety in an NFL secondary. At a time when most defenders had limited attacking skills, sweepers like Franz Beckenbauer showed supreme confidence on the ball and often broke free upfield to lead the offense. But the sweeper position fell out of favor in the early 1990s, replaced by three- and four-man flat back lines that could more easily execute the offside trap by stepping up as a unit to draw opposing attackers offside. That change coincided with the rise of centerbacks who had better technical skills and fullbacks who bombed forward down the flanks. The demise of the classic sweeper made teams more compact—harder to unbalance, easier to move as a unit—and hastened the arrival of modern soccer. So rare is a sweeper sighting at the elite level these days that it was considered shocking when Brazil coach Kleiton Lima deployed a sweeper during the 2011 Women's World Cup.

But what if the *goalkeeper* became the sweeper? That would solve a lot of problems. If the keeper covered more space outside his penalty box, it would allow the back line to move higher and higher up the field, making teams even more compact and forcing the majority of possession closer to the opponent's goal. Beyond his traditional defensive duties, the goalkeeper could also start the attack and serve as a pressure release valve when teammates needed to get rid of the ball. Yes, bringing your goalkeeper out so far presented risks, especially since there was no safety net behind him—just an empty net. But the benefits of the risk were apparent. As early as the 1950s, Hungary's national team goalkeeper, Gyula Grosics, described his role "as a kind of extra sweeper, outside my area" in manager Gusztáv Sebes's attack-minded 4-2-4 formation. (Hungary's "Magnificent Magyars," perhaps the best national team never to win a World Cup, are often viewed as the progenitors of modern soccer.) Around the same time, the legendary Soviet goalkeeper Lev Yashin was introducing innovations that redefined the position as more than merely shot stopping on his line, like starting counterattacks with quick outlets and intercepting passes outside his box. He remains the only goalie ever to win the European Footballer of the Year award (in 1963), and he spawned a line of modern goalkeepers over the years that has included such heirs as Peter Schmeichel, René Higuita, Jorge Campos, Edwin van der Sar, and . . . Manuel Neuer.

You'll notice that there aren't any other German goalkeepers on that list. There have been some outstanding German goalkeepers over the decades, including Jens Lehmann, Oliver Kahn, Harald Schumacher, and Sepp Maier. But they weren't necessarily innovators. "The great German goalkeepers before [Neuer] were extremely pragmatic, and he came out with the flair of catching balls virtually with one hand," says Vincent Kompany, who played for Hamburg from 2006 to 2008 and remembers coming up against a young Neuer when he was the goalkeeper for Schalke. "At first, I think a lot of people, especially in Germany, weren't prepared for his style, his personality. I have always been fascinated by his ability to remain himself in a country that doesn't have a tradition of goalkeepers who behave like him on the pitch."

Kompany says one important factor in Neuer's rise has been his constant improvement, which took another step forward when Pep Guardiola was the Bayern Munich manager from 2013 to 2016. Under Guardiola, the high priest of possession-based soccer, Neuer unlocked the full potential of his abilities to roam far from his goal. "He has this aura about him, which is not typical of a German goalkeeper," Kompany argues. "He's calm and collected. He anticipates the game well. He's good with his feet, and he has improved tremendously. The best thing about a goalkeeper sometimes is just to feel that you can't score, and Neuer has this about him. Van der Sar and Petr Čech have had this aura as well where, before you even take a shot, you feel like you've got less of a chance to score because it's him in goal. It's a presence. These guys fill the goal, and they're not doing it in a clumsy way. They can reach. They can go to the floor. They're like cats, really. I've watched [Neuer's] progression. I've seen him grow from a young kid with many doubters in the beginning, because of his style, to the undoubted number one in the world."

In fact, it's almost alarming how easy it is for elite players to call Neuer the best goalkeeper on the planet. His former Bayern teammate Xabi Alonso even takes his accolades a step further. "From the first day I got here, I was totally impressed by Manuel," says Alonso. "For me, he is the best keeper in football history. I haven't seen anyone control all the situations as well as him. He is good at stopping the ball. He is good at reading the game. He is good with the ball on his feet. He works the space. For me, he is the total goalkeeper. Number one by far." That's saying something, considering Alonso won a World Cup and a Champions League title with renowned Spanish goalkeeper Iker Casillas, who would be on many experts' lists of the top goalkeepers in history.

When Neuer speaks about his goalkeeping influences as a youngster, one revealing aspect is his division between German and non-German keepers and his association of the word *modern* with those who hail from outside Germany. "In Germany, Jens Lehmann was a model style for a German goalkeeper," Neuer says of the player who spent 10 seasons at Schalke, the club that developed Neuer. "In the international style, my idol was [Dutchman] Edwin van der Sar. He was so modern, much more modern than Lehmann. He had another level. He could play with his left and right foot and go out of the box and go out to get crosses. He was present as a personality. Then there was Oliver Kahn: his reflexes, his ambition. He trained hard, and in that sense he was my idol. So I have some different pieces put together. It's like having a lot of coaches, and you save something from the coach that you think is good for you—and that becomes *you*."

Of all the goalkeeper coaches Neuer has had over the years, the one he reveres the most is Toni Tapalović, who was hired by Bayern Munich at Neuer's request when he joined the club in 2011. Like Neuer, Tapalović was born in Gelsenkirchen and played goalkeeper for their hometown club, Schalke. The two men are only five years apart in age, and they developed a connection during Neuer's formative years with the club. "When he was the number two goalkeeper [at Schalke], I was very young," Neuer says. "He knew that I was a little bit better than him, but he always told me that I had to do more. He stayed outside and worked with me when the team was going into the dressing room. And he was my colleague, so we had friendship and cooperation on the pitch. After that, he had a lot of injuries—two shoulders, a knee, the hip—and he stopped his [playing] career and started at Schalke to help the goalkeepers coach. I recommended him to Bayern. I think he has brought me to my best level."

That includes Neuer's sweeper-keeper period, which saw its

full flowering in 2013 and 2014 with the arrival of Guardiola at Bayern and Germany's run to the World Cup title under manager Joachim Löw in Brazil. To hear Neuer tell the story, that glorious month in Brazil was historic for more reasons than one. During the World Cup, he was exposed to the term *sweeper keeper* for the first time. "I had never heard it before," he says with a laugh. "But then at the World Cup they told me what it means, and a newspaper made a picture with the heads of Franz Beckenbauer and mine together, like a collage."

It made for some historic symmetry: Beckenbauer and Neuer, the gold standards of the 20th-century sweeper and the 21st-century sweeper keeper. Innovators. German captains. World Cup champions.

IF THE ALGERIA WORLD CUP game was Neuer's answer to playing Rachmaninoff's Piano Concerto No. 3 at Carnegie Hall, then his childhood goalkeeper training was like learning how to play the scales on his teacher's living-room piano. In most countries, the kids who play goalkeeper are some of the worst athletes on the team; few youngsters actually want to play what is viewed as an unsexy position. (One prominent exception to this rule is the United States, where some of the best athletes go into the goal early, perhaps because the U.S. puts a higher value on the use of the hands in sports.) If you ask around, a lot of the world's top keepers started as children playing other positions on the field. But Neuer, a natural athlete, went against the grain in Germany from the start.

A goalkeeper from the age of four, he discovered early on

that he had a leading foot and a standing leg, and for him it felt more comfortable to jump to his left than to his right in order to make a save. Dives to his right, he says, would often result in awkward landings that gave him bruises on his right hip. Working with a coach, Neuer had to train himself to explode to his right more easily, just as a right-footed player would work on his left foot on the ball.

Even today, Neuer acknowledges that diving and extending his body to his right to stop a shot won't look the same as when he does the same thing diving and extending to his left. "It's the same power, but it looks different because the body changes when you are up in the air," he says. "When you are lying down on the grass and need to stand up, you stand up in a different way on each side. It's not symmetrical. The important thing is that you can jump high and long and stand up quickly. It doesn't have to look so very perfect, but it has to be quick."

Other aspects of basic shot stopping came over time as well, from his positioning on the goal line to covering his near post to staying in front of the ball and keeping his hands in a ready position. (Two hands are always better than one, if possible, when making saves.) Neuer absorbed them all. "The first thing is that I get the ball," he says. "I have to be prepared before the striker comes in my area, and I think the key is to be ready for the shot, to not have any fear, to *know* I can get to the ball. I always want to save it, but just as important for me is that the other players can't get any rebound, any chance to get a goal." During training sessions with Bayern Munich, Neuer is constantly working on drills with Tapalović to hone his reflexes, which can dull quickly otherwise. Being even a split-second slow can make the difference between a goal and a save. Nor does it hurt to face a barrage of shots in training from his Bayern teammates, who are some of the most dangerous finishers in world soccer.

Yet shot stopping, which was once the hallmark of a proficient goalkeeper, is now a bare-minimum requirement. The 21st-century keeper also needs to organize the back line and set-piece defense, command the penalty box on crosses, disrupt opposing forays outside the box, and initiate his own team's attack. Comfort on the ball with both feet is mandatory, as is the ability to unspool passes to moving targets on a dime, over short and long distances, with your feet and with an overhand throw. What's more, the strategic trend of extreme defensive pressing all over the field means goalkeepers often need to make themselves available as pressure-release valves for defenders needing to get rid of the ball. (A 1992 rule change prevented goalkeepers from picking up deliberate back passes, forcing them to use their feet.)

Fortunately for Neuer, he also perfected his foot skills at an early age. When he joined the youth ranks of Schalke as a five-year-old, Neuer would practice with the outfield players when there was no goalkeeper training, developing his favored right foot and weaker left foot, to say nothing of gaining a feel for the complete game. Schalke even considered switching him from goalkeeper to an outfield position when he was 13, the result of concerns that he wasn't as tall as his German youth goalkeeping counterparts. Ultimately, the club decided to keep Neuer in the goal, fully equipped with the tools to redefine the position. (Schalke didn't hold onto him, however: Bayern Munich, as it so often does to its German rivals, poached Neuer for €30 million—$43 million—in 2011.)

"To be a modern goalkeeper, I have to think offensively, to initiate our attacking moves safely and securely," Neuer says.

"Both my teams, Bayern and Germany, usually have more than 60 percent possession. So I have to be outside the box and be involved in the passing game from the back to get the ball to the first, second, and third row of players. All these things are incorporated in my game, but I can afford it because I'm in these strong teams."

If you watch Bayern Munich regularly, it becomes clear that Neuer almost never boots the ball aimlessly downfield, like so many other goalkeepers do. Under Guardiola, the word you heard most often from the Bayern players to describe their attacking philosophy was *control*. Why would you boom the ball downfield and risk giving up control? "The passing game has become more important," Neuer says. "We rarely just hammer the ball forward. I have probably twice as many touches of the ball now than I used to have at Schalke." During the 2015-16 European league season, Neuer completed more passes—in fewer games—than the prolific French striker Antoine Griezmann of Atlético Madrid.

Bayern Munich's and Germany's stranglehold on possession often means Neuer has fewer occasions to demonstrate some of the more traditional goalkeeping skills. But he still has to call upon them at times, knowing that one mistake can turn a game. How does he know when to come out for a cross? The thought process on whether to commit isn't much different from deciding whether to leave his box to cut off a through-ball—though there tends to be more human traffic in his path on crosses, requiring him to read even more variables in a split second. "You have to know which players are in your area and whether you have a free way to get to the ball," he explains. "If I know I can't get the ball, then I have to stay in."

Television commentators sometimes say goalkeepers should always come out for any cross in their 6-yard box. But Neuer argues that's not necessarily the case, noting the size of the smaller box—20 yards by 6 yards, or 1,080 square feet—is still larger than many city apartments. "It depends how high the ball is coming into the box," Neuer says of a cross into his 6. "If it's a high ball they can't reach, you know you can go out. But if it's a very low ball and a striker is there, it's very dangerous and you can't go out." Even today, there are enough variables that the same keeper who'll venture 40 yards from his goal to pick off a ball will sometimes refuse to move even 6 yards, depending on the situation.

More commonly, though, Bayern's and Germany's obsession with control means the ball is at the other end of the field. Neuer says one of the hardest parts of his job is when he hasn't faced a scoring chance by the opposing team in 45 minutes, and then he's suddenly called into action. "Sometimes in the winter it's very cold, you know, especially in Bavaria," he says, half-smiling but fully serious. "It's not easy in this moment, because you have to go from 0 to 100."

Such is life on the German autobahn, soccer division.

BAYERN MUNICH'S TRAINING GROUND ISN'T like the headquarters of most other big European soccer clubs, which tend to be located outside their cities, with heavy security and the distinct feel of compounds designed to keep out the lay masses. Instead, Bayern's compact HQ is on Säbener Strasse, a leafy street in the city of Munich that blends in with its quiet surroundings.

In the tradition of other German clubs, Bayern welcomes its fans on regular occasions to watch training sessions free of charge. It's something you almost never see in, say, the English Premier League. Freshly showered after one of those training sessions, in which fans surrounded the field five deep, Neuer turns to the giant 65-inch video screen in the Bayern Munich boardroom and starts breaking down his clips from a Bundesliga showdown against Borussia Dortmund. As the main challenger to Bayern's dominance in Germany, Dortmund uses a high-pressing defensive style that puts the heat on Bayern's back-line players whenever they have the ball. The idea is to force turnovers in Bayern's own end and take advantage of the quick transition and imbalanced defense to strike quickly.

Neuer and his teammates are prepared for that strategy, of course. In the days before each game, he reviews video clips with Tapalović of his upcoming opponent. "I will see the offensive players who stand out, the attacking style of the team, and the midfielders and defensive players who come forward," he says. Neuer has also been part of the pregame tactical-plan talks with the rest of the squad. Beyond its usual pressing, Dortmund tries to attack Bayern's high back line the same way Algeria did, by sending passes over and through the line into space for the speedy striker Pierre-Emerick Aubameyang. But Neuer keeps an aggressive advanced starting position, and he intercepts a through-ball 35 yards from his goal in the eighth minute before instantly starting the Bayern attack in the other direction. "If I'm in my box and waiting for the ball to come to me, we lose a little bit of time," Neuer says. "If I'm standing higher, we have more time—and Dortmund can't get into the real [defensive] position the way they want."

The *sweeper keeper* is in full effect later when Neuer races out 40 yards from goal to head a piercing through-ball away from Aubameyang's path and directly to teammate David Alaba, who immediately starts a Bayern fast break in the other direction. Ten seconds and three lightning-quick passes later, Bayern has a shot in the Dortmund box. It doesn't go in, but it's one more world-class play by Neuer. While his highlights aren't as breathtaking as in the Algeria game, Neuer is regularly helping Bayern in a new-age way against Dortmund, including serving as a regular passing outlet when his defenders are under pressure.

The little things matter. Before each game, Neuer has a routine as the days progress. He spends time in the gym in advance of every training session as part of his daily physical preparations. These aren't heavy-lifting sessions, but rather routines that prevent injuries during practices, especially as he has grown older. "I'm normally going to 10 to 15 minutes of spinning," he says. "Then I do some stretching and mobilization and stability work that is protection for my body. I'll normally have 25 minutes in the gym, and I feel better." All of Neuer's training sessions are videotaped, and he and Tapalović will pore over his work on individual drills afterward, much as they did during their days at Schalke together. "I will watch my footwork for details and perhaps change something, but just small bits, little nuances," Neuer explains.

Two days before a game, Neuer is looking ahead to the next opponent but also focusing on general work, both individually and with the rest of the team. "With the goalkeepers, we can go for 30 minutes of training with [Tapalović]," Neuer says. "We have some hurdles, and we do some exercises where you jump over them. Then maybe something with the medicine ball and some exercises for the stabilization for your body. We have the strikers out there for shooting and crossing and working on your reflexes. Then we'll have four teams and a small tournament."

In the days before a game, Neuer studies the tendencies of the opponent's set pieces and penalty takers. He's also the one who sets up the Bayern wall to defend free kicks near the goal. For dangerous free kicks, Neuer says, there are plenty of variables that are the goalkeeper's responsibility. "Every team has one or two very good [shooters] on free kicks," he explains. "It always depends on the distance. Some players are better when it's a bit farther out, and in the area close to the box there are some players who have magic feet. It's always different. They also have some tricks: There's a chance they will pass the ball, since they're not always shooting on goal."

One of the hardest things about defending free kicks, Neuer says, is communicating with his teammates who will be in the wall. It's up to him to decide how many players will go into the wall. If there are too few, Neuer won't have enough protection for the side of the goal he's not covering. If there are too many, he'll risk leaving open opposing players who could score off a pass. (One emerging school of thought argues that walls may not even be necessary in some situations.) The Bayern players in the wall "have to pay attention. That is the first thing," he says. "When they don't communicate with you, it's very bad for you. So you can't take your position [as a goalkeeper] right away. You have to be prepared for the kick and have a good feeling."

Penalty kicks happen rarely against Bayern Munich, not least because opponents usually struggle to have possession, especially anywhere near the Bayern penalty box. But Neuer comes to games prepared to deal with penalties anyway. His German goalkeeping idol, Jens Lehmann, famously used handwritten, sweat-stained notes, detailing Argentina's penalty-taking tendencies on a piece of paper that he pulled out of his sock during the World Cup 2006 quarterfinal penalty-kick shootout. (Germany won that shootout, and Lehmann's cheat sheet, now a historic artifact, was later sold for $1.3 million at a charity auction.) More than a decade later, Neuer's spot-kick scouting is done digitally before a game.

"It's on you to prepare yourself [to know] which player can shoot a penalty," he says. "The good thing for the goalkeeper is you don't have so much to lose. The striker has the pressure. It's much easier to be a goalkeeper in that situation." Depending on the league, success rates for teams taking penalties are around 70 percent. Neuer is convinced that he can bring down that percentage by carefully reading every aspect of what happens before the penalty taker strikes the ball. "It starts when he has the ball in his hands and he lays the ball on the ground," Neuer says. "You have to see the position of the ball [on the penalty spot]. Sometimes it will be on the left or the right, on the front or behind. Everyone has their own style. How do they go to the ball? How many steps do they take? What is the body language? Do they go fluently to the ball, or do they stop a little bit? You have to read the whole situation and watch everything. You can't turn around and go clean your gloves or something. It is psychological. It's about being able to read people. If you're not good at reading people, it's not easy. And of course, you can have some luck. The player can choose wherever he wants to go in the last moment, but it's good to do your homework and see how he goes to the ball."

When Dortmund has a corner kick, the onus is on Neuer

to organize Bayern's zonal marking in the box. If you watch enough soccer games on television, you'll hear a maddeningly regular complaint—especially by English commentators—that zonal marking (defending a space, not a particular man) is a terrible way to organize your defense against set pieces, compared to man-to-man marking. This is patent nonsense. *Bad* zonal marking, which allows attackers to get a full running start and leap over the line of defenders, certainly looks awful on TV, as if the defense is actually trying to let the other team score. It's also easier to blame bad zonal marking on the system, rather than on a particular player, as you can easily do with replays showing poor man-to-man marking.

The fact remains that well-executed zonal marking can be more effective than good man marking, which is why Bayern Munich goes zonal when defending corner kicks. (Bayern conceded zero goals on corners in 2016–17 using zonal marking, while Atlético Madrid, another zonal team, gave up only one goal on corners.) The key, Neuer says, isn't just the five Bayern defenders in a horizontal line on the six-yard box, but also the three teammates in a similar line near the penalty spot, whose job is to prevent Dortmund's attackers from getting a running start and leaping over the zone or finding spaces in between. "It's always a zone," he says. "The second line of three players wants to block them so they can't go fast into the zone between the lines."

Just hearing the lingo that Neuer uses while watching video is an education. Here's a snippet from one of our sessions:

ME (*after Neuer starts a buildup from the back*): You're almost never just booting the ball downfield in that situation?

NEUER: No, because Dortmund was in position, and it's better to give a low ball into the feet. We have control, and it makes no sense for us to fast-break.

ME (*as Neuer sets up the Bayern wall to defend a dangerous free kick in the next clip*): What are you communicating to your teammates? What's going on in your head during this moment?

NEUER: First of all, I am at the post, and I speak with the player on the right-hand side of the wall to control the wall and how many players are in it. Now you'll see that I am in my position to see the ball, and I see that there is one player [from Dortmund standing over the ball]. It's only a right foot [to be concerned about]. And now I have to be prepared for what he's doing. I know this player. It's Ilkay Gündoğan, and he plays with me on the national team, so it's very easy for me to be prepared. But if there are two or three players, they can create something, you know? Maybe one player is going over the ball and doesn't touch the ball, and maybe one player is passing and the other is shooting.

ME: When that happens, how does your approach change?

NEUER: Maybe the wall will change. Now I have to speak with the guys to be in the right position. Now I am going to tell Jérôme Boateng that he has to go into the line where Phillip [Lahm], [Robert Lewandowski], [Javi] Martínez, and David Alaba are, because [Boateng] is in my area, and I don't want to have the Dortmund players in my area. Maybe, if I have the chance to get to the ball, Jérôme blocks me, you know? And I tell him to go to the line, to get more space [for myself].

After all that build-up, Gündoğan's free kick is struck poorly and easily cleared by the Bayern defense. But the process of defending it is what's most important, and the player leading that organization is Neuer.

Bayern builds a 2–0 lead against Dortmund before Aubameyang scores on the break late in the first half to make it 2–1. The primary fault is not Neuer's, but how you respond to conceding a goal is also key, he says. "Normally, you know if you can change something or if you have made a mistake. Every time there is something," he says. "But you always have to start again at zero after a goal."

This game, however, is no contest. Bayern goes on to win 5–1, a major victory in its run to another Bundesliga title. Neuer won't make the headlines today, but his performance is terrific—and a direct contrast to that of his Dortmund counterpart, Roman Bürki. The perils of the sweeper keeper are manifold: On two occasions, Bürki allows goals after coming out for the ball and (*whoops!*) missing it.

Being Manuel Neuer is a lot harder than it looks.

IT'S FAIR TO SAY THAT Neuer is the only athlete I have ever interviewed who has brought up the topics of trigonometry and Pythagoras. He did so one day in Munich as we were discussing the essence of goalkeeping. Like Xabi Alonso and Vincent Kompany, Neuer has been forever changed by working under Pep Guardiola as his manager. All three players have continued learning into their 30s under Guardiola, who preaches the gospel of proper positioning. Every square inch of the soccer field matters to Guardiola, who has been known to spend significant portions of his training sessions explaining the difference between standing in spots that are two or three yards apart. These fine details apply not just to field players but to goalkeepers as well.

Just as forwards like Javier Hernández use fixed points as references to gather their bearings on the field—even if Chicharito has his back to the goal, he knows that it's there and won't move—goalkeepers have their own versions of the North Star that help them measure distances and angles in the blink of an eye, as though it were an instinct. "I think the most important basic for the goalkeeper is to have the right position," Neuer says. "Where you have to be is a feeling. You have some marks on the field: the penalty spot, the six-yard box, and the corners of the penalty box. You always have to know where your goal is, and if you are very good in mathematics and trigonometry you can be a good goalkeeper. Pythagoras would have been a good goalkeeper! You feel it, but you have to watch everything. It's not just, 'OK, I have to watch the ball.' You watch the ball, you watch the penalty spot, you watch other things. The penalty spot is always in the middle. It helps me a lot."

Perhaps because the position is so different from the others in soccer, goalkeepers have a kinship that unites them with their counterparts on other teams: the Goalkeepers Union. Even in private conversations with his Bayern Munich teammates, Neuer refuses to slag on another goalkeeper, even if he's from a team that's a bitter rival. "I'm a goalkeeper, and I'll never speak badly about my colleagues," Neuer says. "My teammates always make fun of me because I never say anything about another goalkeeper who makes a mistake. It is the same with my goalkeepers coach. When we watch a game and a striker misses a great chance, I'm not asking [Bayern forward] Thomas Müller why the striker didn't score." The Goalkeepers Union is a brotherhood, and no other position on the field has one. Maybe it has to do with karma, Neuer suggests. "If I am saying something bad about a goalkeeper," he says, "I believe a little bit that it might happen to me."

Neuer can even turn seemingly mundane topics, like equipment, into something intriguing. One day, we get to talking about his preferences on goalie gloves. "First of all, you have to feel comfortable with them," Neuer says. "You have some things that are important for you. The strap must not be too long, because it can't overlap on one side. When it's not fitting, it's not nice to train with. Then the way it's sewn and the connections: I like to have the seams not inside, but outside, so it is a little bit thinner and you have more of a touchy feeling because it's closer, it fits, and it's not so wide. When you have outseams, it is more comfortable, like a ski glove."

The more Neuer talks about his equipment, the more animated he becomes. These are the tools that help him do his job, and he is extremely particular about them. Consider his socks. Neuer likes to wear thicker socks than most goalkeepers wear these days. "Normally, the long socks are very thin now," he says with evident distaste. "The material now, you can say it is much closer to the shoe for you because you have less of it. But growing up with wool socks and tennis socks, this [thicker, padded sock] is much more comfortable for me." Protection—against the weather, against the forces that come with being a goalkeeper— clearly matters to Neuer. During the colder months, he wears two pairs of long, stretchy bicycle pants under a shorter version of the same thing, as well as his uniform. "When I dive and fall to the ground, the skin has to be protected," he explains. "Some goalkeepers start to have problems with their knees." Not even the heat of the Brazil World Cup deterred Neuer from his layers. "Well, it worked!" he says with a smile. "I wear at least three layers all the time. Normally, they make me weigh one-and-a-half kilos more."

One piece of protective gear that Neuer chooses not to wear is a padded helmet of the kind used by the great Czech Premier League goalkeeper Petr Čech. After Čech fractured his skull in 2006 during a collision in a game and underwent surgery, he started wearing the helmet to protect himself from further injury. Even though Čech says he would prefer not to wear the helmet, which limits his hearing ability, he says his medical insurance requires him to do so. "He has to protect it," says Neuer, "but before he had his accidental injury, he never wore it." That's true. But it's also true that European soccer culture's view of head injuries is still one or two decades behind that of the NFL. Neuer's own teammate, Christoph Kramer, suffered a head injury in the 2014 World Cup final and remained on the field for several minutes—risking career-threatening damage—before finally being removed from the game. ("Is this the final?" he asked the referee at one point.)

For his part, Neuer says he has suffered just one significant head injury, which occurred when he was playing for Schalke's reserve team early in his career. A low cross came into Neuer's box, and he came out hard for it. "The striker tried to shoot the ball, but he shot my head," Neuer says. "Then I lost control, and the doctors were with me and said everything was OK. I don't know how much time passed. I had a concussion. And I told them, 'Yes, I can play.' I stood up and laid the ball on the ground, and the referee whistled. I went to take the free kick, and the ball was 2 meters in front of me and I ran through the whole box—15 meters—and left the ball behind. I just ran straight up. The coach took me off, and I said, 'No, no, no.' Everybody was laughing." One hopes they wouldn't be laughing these days, but the global soccer culture still doesn't take head injuries seriously enough.

SOCCER OFFERS MORE FREEDOM TO its players than other sports, in large part because there are no time-outs and players usually have to figure things out during games by themselves. But that's not to say that managers have little influence on their players and how they play the game. In 2016, the Italian manager Carlo Ancelotti—the winner of three Champions League titles—took over for Pep Guardiola at Bayern Munich. And while Ancelotti is famous for tailoring his approach to the skill sets of his players, he still made some significant changes to the way Bayern plays during his year in charge of the club.

Those alterations included an important one at the goalkeeper position. "It seems like I'm not a sweeper keeper as much as I was the last few years," Neuer tells me during one of our conversations in 2017. "Now it is a different game for us. We try to play compact and have a good organization in the defense. But we are not so high on the front line as we were before under Guardiola. We have a little more space up top near the opponents' goal. And we can use the space for our strikers and right and left backs, so that they can overlap and come with crosses. That's the strategy with the new manager." With all of Bayern's lines retreating under Ancelotti, who was fired and replaced by

Jupp Heynckes in October 2017, Neuer had less space to cover behind his back line—and thus fewer sweeper-keeper opportunities to roam outside his penalty box.

"Now I am more the goalkeeper than the sweeper keeper," he says. "There is more regular stuff that I have to do: more saves, more blocks. I can speak much more to my players in front of me because they're closer. I can even reach the midfielders. It was impossible before to reach the midfielders when you shout and try to help them with something. That's different and a new job for me." Neuer took this job seriously. The most common command that he yelled to his teammates, he said, was to create more pressure. At other times, he'd call out another Bayern player's name and let him know there was someone on his right or left shoulder.

Using Opta's statistical database for this book, the analyst Ben Torvaney confirmed what Neuer suspected. Under Guardiola, Neuer's propensity to step up and defend on the front foot was a cut above the rest of the Bundesliga's goalkeepers. Looking at goalkeepers with at least 34 games played (equivalent to a full Bundesliga season) since the start of 2013–14, Neuer immediately stands out. Under Guardiola, Neuer made the second-fewest defensive actions per game—to be expected of a goalkeeper on a possession-controlling team like Bayern—with 7.4. Neuer also had the highest proportion of his defensive actions taking place outside the penalty box at 4.1 percent. Things changed, however, under Ancelotti. In his 26 league games in 2016–17, Neuer's proportion of defensive actions made outside the box plummeted to 1.7 percent. What was remarkable about Neuer was his ability to slip so fluently back into a more traditional goalkeeping role.

While Neuer's proactive defending was scaled back for Bayern Munich, Torvaney notes that we didn't see as drastic a change in his output on the ball. The proportion of passes received outside the box has remained relatively steady, going from 39.5 percent under Guardiola to 38.1 percent in 2016–17 under Ancelotti. Likewise, the proportion of his touches on the ball that comprise goalkeeper-specific actions (catches, saves, etc.) increased from 16.4 percent to 18.0 percent. Being able to contribute to the team when in possession is part of what makes Neuer so versatile, so it wasn't surprising that Ancelotti continued to leverage it for his team's benefit.

Neuer said he wasn't disappointed that Ancelotti curtailed his sweeper-keeper feats. He argued that, even though he gets fewer touches with his feet during Bayern's buildup, he liked making more saves. How he performed in games under Ancelotti was closer to the drills he did in training than was the case during Guardiola's tenure. Besides, he added, German national team coach Joachim Löw still asks him to perform a lot of the sweeper-keeper tasks that Guardiola demanded. "With Germany we play a bit like the system with Pep," Neuer said, "and we try to push the ball and the other team back, to have a small distance to the [opposing] goal, to get the ball very early on the counterattack. I think Germany is between Carlo and Pep, but more on the Pep side."

Ancelotti may have wanted Neuer to play differently than he did under Guardiola, but the manager still trusted his goalkeeper implicitly. With the retirement of Philipp Lahm, Neuer became Bayern's captain at the start of the 2017–18 season, just as he took over the armband for the German national team in 2016 after the international retirement of Bastian Schweinsteiger. When you're the world's best goalkeeper and you have raised the most important trophies in the sport—the World Cup and the UEFA Champions League—you're always looking for the next challenge to show you're not satisfied. For Neuer, that means becoming a better leader and—yes, it's possible—a better goalkeeper. "I always want to do a better job, to get everything out of my body, to train well, and I never get tired of it," Neuer says. "We won the Champions League with Bayern. We won the World Cup with Germany. But we're still hungry, and that's me as well."

Neuer's international legacy is already secure, not just in his individual and team accolades but also in his redefinition of the goalkeeper position. But it's also clear that he is leaving a *domestic* legacy, too, in Germany. Younger German goalkeepers in their 20s, like Marc-André ter Stegen (Barcelona) and Kevin Trapp (Paris Saint-Germain)—aren't known for their pragmatism, as Neuer's predecessors were, but rather for having more modern keeper skill sets, from their attacking distribution to their serial risk taking to their dynamic defending of areas outside the penalty box.

"There are a lot of good young German goalkeepers, and I think it's easier today to become a better goalkeeper," Neuer says. "The coaches and the game are more modern. You see it at the professional level. Keepers play with both feet. They can play outside the box and in the goal. They don't have so many weaknesses, like you saw 20 years ago. They have the complete package. Goalkeepers coaches don't just work on one thing now. They work on everything, and it's easier to become a better goalkeeper."

That much is certain. Whether anyone will become another Manuel Neuer is another question entirely.

5

THE MANAGER

Roberto Martínez's Constant Adaptation

"It is only when you meet someone of a different
culture from yourself that you begin to realize
what your own beliefs really are."

—George Orwell, *The Road to Wigan Pier*

THE TRAINING CENTER OF THE ROYAL BELGIAN FOOTBALL
Association is in Tubize, a quiet town southwest of Brussels,
where the stars of one of the world's most talented national
teams can stay in a sparkling new luxury hotel right next to
the well-tended practice grounds, far from the distractions of
the big city. Blessed with a generation of players unlike any the
country has produced before, Belgium has stocked English Premier League clubs with some of their most reliable performers,
from Manchester City (Vincent Kompany, Kevin De Bruyne)

to Manchester United (Romelu Lukaku, Marouane Fellaini), from Chelsea (Eden Hazard, Thibaut Courtois) to Tottenham Hotspur (Jan Vertonghen, Mousa Dembélé, Toby Alderweireld). On paper, Belgium has enough dazzling talent to win the World Cup. In *practice*, however, the Red Devils have been far less than the sum of their parts, the cardinal sin of coaching, which explains why a new manager is here on a sunny April morning in Tubize.

The failure to fulfill expectations has come to define Belgium in recent years. Under the beleaguered Belgian Marc Wilmots, who managed the national team from 2012 to 2016, the Red Devils appeared to have an open path to the final of Euro 2016, but they came up woefully short, losing 3–1 to Wales in the quarterfinals. Afterward, Belgian goalkeeper Courtois complained publicly about Wilmots's refusal to change his tactics after an earlier defeat in the tournament to Italy. It was one thing to fail the first time against a team with a 3-5-2 formation, Courtois argued, but to commit the same fatal mistakes against another 3-5-2 team was inexcusable. Wilmots's bosses agreed. Soon he was out the door, replaced by a coach whose eagerness to adapt—to new countries, strategies, and ways of thinking— has defined his career.

In 1995, at the age of 21, Roberto Martínez moved from his native Spain to Wigan, a town in northwest England, known mainly for Orwell's chronicle of its harsh living conditions in the 1930s. Martínez joined Wigan Athletic, and over 10 years—6 as a midfielder and, later, 4 as a manager—he helped make Wigan famous for something else: punching above its weight class in English soccer. During its eight seasons in the Premier League from 2005 to 2013, no team produced less revenue than Wigan

Athletic. Based on the club's salary bill, in fact, the authors of *The Numbers Game* calculated that Wigan's chances of being relegated at some point from the Premier League over the five seasons from 2007–08 to 2011–12 were 95 percent. Yet, somehow, the Latics stayed up. Every season they were better than the sum of their parts. For Martínez, who managed Wigan from 2009 to 2013, survival depended on the axiom *Adapt or die.*

Part of that process involved his soccer philosophies, which melded his Spanish upbringing with the lessons he acquired over two decades in the British game. "I'm a product of my own experiences," Martínez says during one of our interviews over a two-year period. "I left my homeland in '95 and had to learn English. The different cultures of the game have always been in my head. You learn quickly that there's no right or wrong in football. My education comes through a game based in possession, on wanting to have the ball, and the difficulties of breaking a team down and being brave in possession. Over my time in the U.K., I needed to adapt to what's needed in the British game. You need to cope with dead-ball situations because they're so important. The physicality and strategy behind those are a big influence in scorelines. Then the incredible dynamism when you lose possession is a big difference from the physicality in other leagues around the world. So it's a combination of influences."

Martínez's willingness to adapt extended to his shifting tactics from season to season, too. In pure philosophical terms, he prefers a style that stresses possession and produces goals from open play, not set pieces. (Martínez even thinks the rules should be changed to award 0.5 goals for a dead-ball strike and 1.0 goals for those scored from the run of play.) But in practice he has shown a tendency to go with what works when necessary.

In 2010–11, Martínez's Wigan managed to stay in the Premier League by scoring almost four times as many goals from free kicks as the league's average team and twice as many goals on counterattacks. During the 2011–12 season Martínez changed things up again, switching from his usual 4-3-3 formation (rare in the Premier League) to an even more exotic 3-4-3 for the final third of the campaign as Wigan stayed up again. Even though reality caught up to the Latics the following season, when they were relegated, Martínez still led Wigan to the remarkable achievement of winning the FA Cup for the first time, beating Manchester City in the final. He moved to Everton the following season, finished a surprising fifth in the Premier League, and signed a new five-year contract, certifying his reputation as one of the hottest talents in coaching.

By then, Martínez had become a familiar face in the United States after trying something new: working for ESPN as a television analyst for the World Cup (in 2010 and 2014) and the European Championship (in 2012 and 2016). The affable Spaniard was a natural in front of the camera, dispensing clear insights with a zest for the game that's contagious. To hear him say it, the Martínez that Americans have gotten to know on television is essentially the same guy as Martínez the manager. "I enjoy the challenge of being in front of an audience that is not too familiar with the sport," he explains. "I like being as open as I can and trying to make things as simple to understand as I can. As a manager, I'm the same way. The only thing you should add is that, as a manager, you need to be very much aware of the standards of *others* around the work, and that's the part that you don't show on television. In television, it's very focused on the concepts and the tactical aspects of the game, and how you read the game. I like that sort of in-depth analysis in the day-to-day work of a manager as well."

Martínez's enjoyment while talking soccer is palpable; his hands cut through the air as he speaks in a rat-a-tat rhythm in lightly Spanish-inflected English. His thinning dark hair is trimmed more closely to his scalp than it was during his Everton days. It serves to highlight his eyebrows, which dance and furrow, depending on whether he's deep in thought or wide-eyed over a story he's sharing. If you ask him which managers have influenced him the most, Martínez mentions four men from four different countries. He says he fell in love with the swashbuckling style of Barcelona's "Dream Team" in the early 1990s, managed by the Dutch legend Johan Cruyff. He was fascinated by the attention to detail of the Italian Arrigo Sacchi, who coached AC Milan's European Cup–winning teams of the late 1980s and early 1990s. He also cites the bravery and attacking flair of Francisco Maturana's Colombia national team of the early 1990s and the use of young players by the Welshman John Toshack at Spain's Real Sociedad, where his teams played with what Martínez calls an "incredible arrogance."

It's clear from the smile on Martínez's face that he considers *arrogance* to be a compliment. "Absolutely," he says. "Being arrogant on the pitch means you are yourself. You can express yourself on the ball. In football there are two rules: one, that you're trying to create and, two, that you're trying to keep a clean sheet. It's a lot easier to knock a building down than it is to build it. If you're not arrogant, you're not going to build a good product. That's where the arrogance comes. Arrogance where you show for

the ball when the whole crowd is against you, or when you're losing 1–0 and you should be winning. That's a real sense of arrogance, that you need to keep showing yourself and keep showing
resilience when the easiest thing would be to hide and look away."

Martínez has had to demonstrate his own resilience in recent years. He was still at Everton when we started our interviews for this book, but a Premier League manager has one of
the least secure jobs in sports. There are outliers like Sir Alex
Ferguson, who stayed at Manchester United for 27 years, and
Arsène Wenger, who took over Arsenal in 1996. But at the start
of 2018 the longest-tenured Premier League manager other than
Wenger was Bournemouth's Eddie Howe, who was in just his
sixth season on the job. When Martínez was fired by Everton in
May 2016—the Toffees ended up having consecutive 11th-place
league finishes—it was one more sacking in a season that saw
José Mourinho pushed out by Chelsea just seven months after
he had won the Premier League title. As every manager knows,
getting fired is part of the job in the modern game.

For his part, Martínez has strong feelings about the lack of
patience with Premier League managers, and those are tied to
what he views as the differing job descriptions between a *manager* (the term used most frequently in England) and a *head coach*
(a term employed more often on the Continent). "We get confused at times," Martínez says. "In Italy and Spain and France,
they work with *head coaches*, and then you have the figure of *director of football* [who's responsible for such tasks as long-term
strategy and player signings]. A head coach is just responsible for
the first-team results, so it's only fair that if you lose three games
in a row your position is going to be in question. As a *manager*,
it's different. You're managing the short term, the mid term, and

the long term of the football club. You need to have that strategy very clear: how you're going to use the finances, how you're going to develop the team, how you're going to play, how you're going to allow young players to have opportunities and a clear path into the first team. So clearly that [job security] should not rely on three bad results. But [Premier League] positions are so volatile that, unfortunately, they're going to affect big calls that could help the football club in the long term, especially with young players. The stats are there to show that fewer and fewer managers will make long-term decisions." Some Premier League clubs do have a genuine director of football, including Manchester City, Chelsea, Liverpool, and Southampton. But others remain dominated by old-style managers: Manchester United, Arsenal, and West Ham United.

Yet just as Mourinho found another coveted job quickly (at Manchester United), Martínez landed the Belgium position in August 2016 (after turning down interest from the Premier League and China). Not long after Euro 2016, the technical committee of the Belgian federation asked to meet with Martínez about its open coaching job. Though Martínez had always been intrigued by the possibility of managing a national team someday, he thought that would be some years off. At age 43, he enjoyed the breakneck pace of managing in the club game and still had plenty of energy to do it. But the more he thought about the Belgium opportunity and the chance to do something historic with all that talent, the more he sold himself on the job. How many national teams could reach consecutive quarterfinals at World Cup 2014 and Euro 2016 and have those be considered disappointments? If everything came together, this Belgium team could raise the trophy at Russia 2018.

What's more, the man known for a career of adaptations saw an enticing challenge in moving to another new culture and coaching Belgian players who had been forced to adapt in their own ways to a country with three official languages and a wide variety of playing styles. "That was quite intriguing for me," Martínez says over coffee one day in Tubize. "I had been working with Romelu Lukaku, Kevin Mirallas, and Marouane Fellaini—three Belgian players—but they were so different that that was always something in the back of my mind, to try to understand how so much diverse talent comes together in the same nation. Then you've got up to 25 Belgian players in the British game, so I had a close understanding of these players."

The role of a national team coach is far different from that of a club manager, and spending time with Martínez in both his Everton and Belgium jobs allows us to explore the differences (and similarities) in detail. What you'll also see clearly is that Martínez's willingness to make big changes in his life is of a piece with his willingness to make big changes in his teams as a manager. He is influencing Belgium, just as Belgium is influencing him. "Traveling is part of my life," he says. "I left home at 16, and then I left my country at 21, and now I'm in a new country learning a new culture. This is almost like going back to when I was 21. I've found out that I'm a curious person, and I'll carry on doing that until the day I die."

IN A TRADITIONAL, ENGLISH-STYLE SYSTEM, a club manager is responsible for five main tasks. The first one involves partici-

pating in the roster formation for the first team and the devel-
opmental teams below. Other actors will be involved, including
the club owner(s), the board, the manager's assistant coaches,
and the scouting department, which in modern soccer is usually
aided by a staff whose role is to provide data analysis of prospects from around the world. Yet it is the manager who is in
charge of developing an identity and a preferred playing style, as
well as the strategies to achieve those objectives over the short,
medium, and long term.

The second task is to prepare the first-team players for games.
That includes organizing training sessions and giving the players the information they need to know how to perform against
a particular opponent. It also involves managing personalities
and egos, especially among the players who aren't chosen for the
starting lineup. (You'll recall Javier Hernández saying that Manchester United manager Sir Alex Ferguson was a master at this
task.) The third function of a club manager is to arm himself
with information before a game about his players (and his opponent's players) that might help in making decisions. The fourth
task is to manage his players during the game, which involves
making substitutions and tactical switches, as well as giving
team talks before and after the game and at halftime.

The fifth function is to serve as the public face of the team in
regular interactions with the media. In recent years, this aspect
of the job has become more important and time-consuming
than ever. No sports league in the world has done more than
the Premier League to build interest through the story lines and
mind games (with players, managers, and referees) that emerge
from this ready-made theater, equal parts Shakespearian and

Machiavellian. In the high-stakes world of European club soccer, a clever manager can take pressure off his players through what he says in the media. More than ever before, there is value in winning the press conference.

Yet when managers (and those who are hoping to be managers) talk about the "work," they aren't referring to media interviews, but rather to the daily craft of the job, from player acquisition to preparation, from strategy sessions to interpersonal relations with the players. During his 19-year career as a midfielder, Xabi Alonso played under some of the game's great managers: Pep Guardiola, Carlo Ancelotti, José Mourinho, Vicente del Bosque, Rafa Benítez, and Luis Aragonés. In 2014, Alonso asked for a transfer from Real Madrid to Bayern Munich so that he could prepare for his next career as a manager by learning from the famously obsessive Guardiola. Toward the end of Alonso's second and final season with Guardiola, I asked him what makes Guardiola so special as a manager, and his answer dealt directly with Guardiola's day-to-day work inside the team.

"You see that he is great as a manager," Alonso said. "He deals with that leadership position really well. He knows how to connect with the players. He has that passion to have an empathy with the player. That's very important. One-on-one, he is really persuasive. He convinces you in a smooth way, and that's the best way to convince someone. From the football point of view, he is brave enough to make the decisions that would scare someone. I really admire that. He wants to try new things, always thinking: What can we do to get better? He doesn't just take things for granted. Apart from all those qualities, he is a great worker."

For Alonso, adaptation is an essential component of a first-rate manager, especially one who has come into a new job. In

2016, Guardiola was replaced at Bayern Munich by Ancelotti, who had also coached Alonso to a Champions League title at Real Madrid. But when I asked Alonso if Ancelotti's Bayern Munich would play differently than his teams at Real Madrid, Alonso nodded vigorously. "It's not about the manager, it's about the *players*," he said. "You know Ancelotti. He has been in so many clubs. He's wise enough to know the players and get the best from them. For example, the game of [Bayern midfielder] Thiago is not the same as the game of [Real Madrid's Ángel] Di María, who I used to play alongside in Madrid with Ancelotti. You need to adapt and work the best possible way with the players that you have."

Few players will ever have the luxury that Alonso enjoyed of working with so many managing greats. Nor do many players go to the lengths that Alonso did to learn about the craft of managing, knowing that he wanted to become a manager himself eventually. In the final years of his playing career, Alonso prepared for his next step as a manager by keeping a notebook of observations—"not on the iPad, but in an old-school notebook," he said, using one of his favorite expressions—from the training ground, the locker room, and the video theater. He also made sure to write down lessons that had stuck with him from earlier in his career, choices that he wanted to make his own on the sideline or the practice field someday. *Principles*, he called them. How he wanted his teams to play. How to achieve *control*, Guardiola's single most important buzzword. How to anticipate playing against a four- or five-man back line. How to deal with a team pressing you with one or two strikers. And then the big stuff: how to form an identity as a manager and build relationships with players.

It was all there in Alonso's notebook, carefully written by hand. He had won the World Cup, had won the Champions League and La Liga and the Bundesliga, and yet he always viewed himself as a craftsman. Now he was approaching becoming a manager the same way. In doing so, Alonso saw himself less as an elite athlete and more as an apprentice in a trade trying to take the next step. Gathering ideas in his notebook, he said, "is something that people tend to do in many other jobs or areas. Like an architect or a scriptwriter. You take notes whenever you see a good idea. And sometimes you have those ideas in your mind, but to put them in writing makes them more clear and makes you more sure of them. For me it works, and not just for the short term but especially for the long term. Hopefully they will be useful. I don't know what is going to happen, but it is better to get ready for that."

Guardiola had filled Alonso's notebook with so much information on the details of positioning that, in his 30s, Alonso felt like a kid in grade school again. Every day with Guardiola brought something new. "He loves the positional football," Alonso marveled. "He might be showing us one 15-minute video of Mario Götze just standing in his [forward] position, waiting. And he loves that. You have to be willing to do nothing sometimes. You are just standing here waiting, because they have a job, and your job is to be there at the end and get the ball. You do nothing. Just wait. He shows that and you visualize it. On the pitch you are not aware of that, but once you watch the video, you see why at the end the machine works. Because the pieces are in the right place, and they work at the right time. That's something that I really enjoy watching."

When Guardiola moved to Manchester City in 2016, he began

having a similar effect on Vincent Kompany, who might also go into coaching after finishing his playing career. For Kompany, working daily with Guardiola is like taking a doctorate-level course in soccer. And now that Kompany has worked with Roberto Martínez, both for ESPN and for Belgium, he says he sees a kinship between the two Spanish managers. "I knew [Martínez] a little from before he was the manager with the national team," Kompany says. "There are a lot of similarities between him and Pep Guardiola. Tactically, [Martínez] pays attention to detail, and he has a very good education and background in the game. I think he tries to apply a positive way of playing football that suits the needs of big teams."

To Martínez, that means exerting control over the game through possession, breaking down defensive-minded opponents, and giving his players a tactical framework that maximizes their freedom to use their many talents and make big plays. Adaptation and flexibility are priorities. From a club perspective, Martínez says, "Your philosophy needs to adapt to the players that you have and to the role of the football club in relation to the other clubs, and then you come up with a very own identity of your team. That philosophy comes down to being technically gifted as a side, so you can control the football, and being flexible tactically. You should be able to cope with different systems and be able to give players the opportunity to think and make their own decisions."

Every manager has a style in dealing with players and teams. During his legendary tenure at Manchester United, Sir Alex Ferguson was notorious for his "hair dryer" outbursts in the locker room, so named because they figuratively scorched their underachieving recipients until they performed better. Ferguson's approach worked, not least because it represented an authentic side of him. Putting the fear of God into his players is not part of Martínez's style or personality. He says there are so many emotional ups and downs as a manager that you have to be yourself in the job. If you try to be someone you're not, he argues, things will fall apart during periods of adversity. An article of faith for Martínez is that his teams will be better than the sum of their parts if he manages them through aspiration as opposed to denigration.

"I have never believed in managing through punishment, or having the stick, or forcing a player to perform in a certain manner," Martínez says, "because I don't think you can achieve a dream that way. You can just reach your level, and that's it. And the more you turn away or you drop your awareness, the more players will drop their standards. I have always felt that you need to trust the players to have the same aspirations as a team, and that becomes very powerful. That can bring a momentum which can allow you to achieve things beyond a sum of individuals. So you give a big responsibility to every player in that dressing room and manage through the aspiration of achieving something as a team. Some players may drop their standards and have that affect their profession, and as a manager you've got the job, unfortunately, of getting rid of those players that are not going in the direction of the aspiration of the group."

Management through aspiration worked extremely well for Martínez at Wigan, which stayed in the Premier League far longer than anyone expected and won a stunning FA Cup title. The results were more mixed at Everton, and now Martínez is pointing Belgium—easily the most talented squad he has ever coached—toward the biggest knockout tournament of them all, the World Cup. Martínez's teams tend to do well in knockout tournaments. He won the FA Cup, and he even took Everton to the semifinals of the FA Cup and the League Cup during the season he was fired. If he can inspire Belgium to be greater than the sum of its parts, well, the rest of the world had better look out.

Ultimately, Martínez says, there are no tricks of the trade when it comes to managing. Each team is different and requires an individual approach. "Your group could be players with an incredible work rate, or it could be a group of incredible talent but not a huge work rate," he says. "You could have players that have been damaged from previous experiences or players that are full of energy, full of bravery, full of dreams. Every group is different, and the quicker you understand that group, the quicker you can affect that group. How you do it is down to its own particular moment."

One thing that never changes, according to Martínez, is the demanding nature of the job. There is no such thing as a work-life balance for managers, he says, especially if you want to keep working. "That's what young coaches need to get straight away," he explains. "Being a manager is not a job. It's a way of living. It has to be a passion. The moment you get into this job thinking, 'When am I going to get a day off?' Or, 'When am I going to get that time that I can be enjoying myself?' It doesn't exist. You're not going to last in this business. And the quicker that someone tells you that, the better, because otherwise you're going to end up suffering a lot. The moment that you take it just as a job, you're not going to do everything that you should have done to help the players win a game."

How consuming is soccer for Martínez? A few years ago, he and his Scottish wife, Beth, found that on the rare evenings when Roberto was home from the training ground, he would end up watching soccer in a separate room of the house while she watched something else in the living room. Their solution? They bought an L-shaped sofa for their living room and installed two televisions on perpendicular walls. "So we can be sitting together," Roberto explains, "but I'm watching my football on TV here and she's watching her soap here—with her volume on, obviously, because she's the boss in the house. If the football is really interesting I've got the headphones on, but if not I'll watch the football with no sound."

He smiles. Even the finest coaching careers are marked by just a few strokes of genius. That may have been one of them.

THE NAMES OF THE CLUB training grounds in the English Premier League sound a lot like country estates or a new line of upmarket products sold at Restoration Hardware. The list includes Cobham (Chelsea), Melwood (Liverpool), and Colney (Arsenal). Finch Farm, Everton's leafy 55-acre training ground southeast of Liverpool, has facilities for the first team and the youth academy, an indoor practice field, 10 full-size grass fields, and an exact replica of the pitch at the club's modest stadium, Goodison Park. On a brisk Friday afternoon in January 2016, Roberto Martínez is deep inside Finch Farm headquarters, watching video with me of Everton's wild 3–3 tie against Chelsea at Stamford Bridge from two weeks earlier.

As we start, I ask him an open-ended question: *When you watch a game, whether it's on video or in person, what are you looking for as a manager that the average fan might not notice?* Martínez doesn't hesitate. "Numerical advantage," he says. "Goals happen because you get a numerical advantage in that position, or because someone makes a mistake. You can't prepare for someone to make a mistake, so what you have to prepare for is to create a 1v1 situation, a 2v1 situation, a 2v2, a 3v3. If you can create a 3v3 situation, with the quality that we have in the Premier League, that will end up in the back of the net. It's very rare, so you need to find a way to do that. In the same way, you need to see *why* when you've been left at a numerical disadvantage. What has the opposition done? It could be just a lucky flick-on, or someone goes for a 50/50 ball and loses it. But if it's a fullback having a really good starting position high up and combining with a winger, then you need to try to assess that as it happens."

Martínez is always searching for something else, too. "The other aspect that you look for constantly is that the players are doing what they're good at well," he says. "I would never [focus on] a player doing something badly, because that's part of the game. The game is going to force you to make errors, and you play with your feet, so you're going to make mistakes. It's stating the obvious to someone to say, 'Oh, he crossed it out of play.' You're never going to get anything out of highlighting that. But if you see someone who's an outstanding dribbler and he *doesn't* take that opportunity to take people on, then there's something wrong. I always reduce everything to players performing at the level that they are expected to by doing good things well, and then numerical advantages for and against. That's what you're quickly assessing all the time."

When Martínez is managing during a game, he prefers to stand in his coach's box by himself, away from his team and staff on the bench. During his first managerial job, at Swansea City, he says, he would sit down for the first 10 minutes but inevitably decide to stand up anyway. There were too many distractions sitting down, from one assistant saying their defenders weren't marking tightly enough to another assistant arguing that they weren't throwing enough bodies forward. For Martínez, the coaching box is what he calls a "safe area," where he can focus on seeing the game and sensing the emotion, intensity, and energy levels of his players. All coaches have their preferences and tics. The former U.S. men's national team coach Bob Bradley once told me that as he watches games, he envisions an imaginary light bulb above each of the players on the field and values those players whose light bulbs are turned on for as much of the 90 minutes as possible.

When Martínez is watching games on video, he's particular about the way he consumes them. He doesn't want to view the broadcast presentation that most fans consume, which includes lots of player close-up shots and instant replays. Instead, Martínez prefers viewing a wide-angle shot of the whole field—the so-called tactical cam—which allows him to see all 22 players and how they move into space, with and without the ball. Oftentimes, what is happening *away* from the ball is the key to a successful action on the field. It may be hard to believe, but Martínez says he watches every game a total of 10 times afterward, the better to see the perspectives of each of his 10 field players during the 90 minutes.

"Otherwise, you miss something," he says, insisting that the 15 hours are worth it, even given his limited time. "After watching it 10 times, you come up with different assessments. Sometimes you see an action and you want to watch it 5 or 6 times from everyone to understand it. But if you watch a game from one player's position, you see the game in a completely different manner and you can understand his decisions a lot better. So when you watch an action in isolation, I would say, 'Why is he covering so much? Why is he not with him?' But when you watch a whole 90 minutes and you see it from his perspective, you'll see on the three actions before that he got tight twice and his man got past him too easily. His natural way of coping with that is giving [his man] an extra three yards, even though that affected his position with the center-half. So it gives you a better understanding of the decision making of the players."

One major difference in preparing a club team instead of a national team is the sheer volume of matches at the club level. There are 38 games in a Premier League season, in addition to the FA Cup and the League Cup knockout tournaments and possible European competition in the Champions League or Europa League. In their preparations for the Chelsea-Everton league game, Martínez and his staff had to view the match in the context of playing five games in a 14-day cycle. That meant making changes in the starting lineup from game to game. "The days of playing with 11 players are gone," Martínez says. "You used to have 12 players, and if you had an injury, you had someone else coming in. Now you need to use 22, 23 players, and anyone can play. A player cannot play three games in seven days. It's impossible. The other thing is bearing in mind who you play in the Premier League. You need to be aware of the quality of the goal-scoring threat of the opposition. So you have to be flexible to have consistent results, which is a bit of a contradiction. But it's the nature of the modern game."

Here's another contradiction: It's a hoary cliché in sports that you take things one game at a time—which Martínez insists that his players still must do—but in club management you have to prepare for blocks of games or your squad will be overwhelmed. For its part, the medical staff focuses on players' recovery and keeps close tabs on their physical performance metrics in training and in games. (Martínez notes that the injury risk for players skyrockets whenever they exceed 3,000 to 3,500 minutes played in a season.) At Everton, Martínez's analysis department, which included traditional scouts and more modern data analysts, worked well ahead to prepare reports on the team's next six opponents, usually three at home and three away. You don't want to analyze a team too far in advance, though, or you might miss some important new intel. And, Martínez cautions, you don't want to rely too much on data that could lead you astray. "We've got too much data," he says. "The problem isn't data. The problem is how you question and interrogate with that data. I would say that I only use data to solve an instinct. If I've got an instinct or a doubt that comes from my assessment, that is when I use data to back it up. I've found over the years that that's the most powerful way to use data. If you just put data floating against data, it can take away from what all this cannot see, which is your work with the players on the training ground." In the end, the goal of the preparation and analysis reports is to be granular and exhaustive in producing a "clear X-ray," as Martínez puts it, of an opponent's strengths and weaknesses so that you can build a game plan for them.

"Every team prepares in a different manner," Martínez says. "There are teams that are very much concerned about what *they* do, and they don't pay any attention to the opposition. Other teams, because they are so concerned about building their success on being very strong defensively and keeping clean sheets, most of their preparation goes on the strengths of the *opposition*. I'm very much about preparing the team on what *we're* going to do, and how good we can be with what we do, and then having a real good awareness of the opposition. I think our way of preparing for games is the hardest one and the most time-consuming. We're working a lot in every training session to prepare our way of playing, what we're going to expect from the threat of the opposition, and how we're going to exploit their weaknesses."

In the thick of a Premier League season, though, when you're dealing with injuries and fatigue, and the games come fast and furious, Martínez says the ideal preparation plan doesn't always match up to the reality of the situation. If you have games on a Wednesday and Sunday, he explains, some players will only be able to recover for the 48 hours after the Wednesday game, which means they can work on little more than video preparation on Thursday and Friday. Once they return to the training field on Saturday, Martínez says, he typically has them go through only a half-session with a game taking place the next day.

After Martínez puts together his starting lineup for the Chelsea-Everton game, he encounters what he calls the most difficult part of his job: telling a player that he isn't among the 11 players starting the game. "You put a squad together of 24 different careers and different brains to become a winning team, and the reality is only 11 can start," he says. "As a manager, you need to make decisions that are for the good of the team to try and win a game, but that doesn't mean the individual will agree in the same manner. And that's the hardest thing as a manager: to disappoint a player who you know has been working well and is going to be very important through the course of the season." Some managers reveal the starting lineup to their teams the day before the game. But Martínez's policy is to wait until the last possible moment 90 minutes before kickoff. There are several reasons, he says. One, the later you leave it, the more you can prepare for the unexpected, like a player falling ill or picking up an injury in training the day before the game. Two, Martínez wants every player to come to work on game day thinking he's going to play, whether his role is as a starter or a substitute. And three, he says being ready to play is part of being a professional.

Communication is key, though, Martínez explains, especially with players who don't make the lineup. "Sometimes you speak with them before you announce the team," he says, "and then if there's anything specifically you want them to work on, or a specific role they need to have, they need to be told. If a player expected to play and there is a reason, apart from not performing well, you have to make them aware and tell them. And you tell them just before you make the final presentation."

Remember Martínez's discussion above about numerical advantage being the key factor that leads to goals? He and his staff spend hours in advance of each game studying their opposition analysis reports as well as their own team's performances to come up with a strategic game plan for the match and a few tactical instructions. Those directives are intended to give his team numerical advantages and prevent such advantages for the opponent. The process takes time. There are no easy answers, and Martínez can find himself stuck without a solution until he has—voilà!—a eureka moment. His goal, he says, is always to come up with a tactical advantage to the opposition and share that plan with his players. During the game, it's up to the players to use their talent in their own ways to apply that tactical advantage within the framework that Martínez has presented.

As we watch the opening minutes of the Chelsea-Everton game, Martínez reveals one of Chelsea's defensive weaknesses that he and his staff identified heading into the game: right back Branislav Ivanović's lack of awareness, which Everton is hoping to exploit to create one-on-one situations (a numerical advantage in Martínez's world) with Everton forward Kevin Mirallas going against Chelsea's right centerback Kurt Zouma. The plan, Martínez says, is for Mirallas to play in the space behind Ivanović, who will often be out of position and unable to double up on Mirallas when he gets the ball and moves to take on Zouma one-on-one. "Ivanović has a big problem with anything that is happening in his back, because he hasn't got a big awareness," Martínez says, motioning to the screen. "So if you play with a player here [behind Ivanović] and a player here [out wide], he'll make the wrong call. So we had a player, Kevin Mirallas, who would play behind him."

On the screen, you can see Everton trying to create the advantage from the opening whistle. "See, [goalkeeper] Tim Howard has the ball, and he knows that we're going to be playing behind that space," Martínez says. "So the ball goes to [midfielder] Mo Běsić, and he's already looking for that advantage. We're trying to get [Mirallas and Zouma] 1v1, and we got that six times. One ended up with a corner that we scored from, and the other five, to be fair, Zouma was outstanding." He points to the screen again. "See, [Zouma and Ivanović] are arguing already. You look for areas where you give direction to the players without taking away the natural creative approach of an individual."

On the defensive side, Martínez says, his instructions include a directive on dealing with Willian, Chelsea's right-sided midfielder, who has been one of his team's few bright spots in a brutal season that has already seen the firing of Mourinho as manager. Willian is a constant threat with his dribbling, so Martínez has asked his players to make sure Willian is never in a one-on-one situation when he receives the ball. Everton, like Chelsea, is playing in a 4-2-3-1 formation, so Martínez assigns left defensive midfielder Běsić to mark Willian along with left fullback Leighton Baines. On the screen, Chelsea passes the ball to Willian on the right side, and Běsić moves over to create a 1-on-2 situation. "Defensively, [Běsić] knows that he needs to help [Baines] with Willian," Martínez says. "So straight away you can see that the instruction is there, that [Běsić] understood the instruction and it's working. But sometimes you can have an instruction that opens you up in another area. You may stop Willian, but then [his teammate] Cesc [Fàbregas] has got space. So you need to constantly reassess that what you're doing is working in a game."

If an opponent is extremely strong defensively, Martínez says, he may give up to four instructions like the one above to take advantage of Ivanović and create one-on-one situations with Mirallas and Zouma. But if the opponent isn't strong defensively, there may be only one directive. Whether you're talking about Martínez's offensive and defensive instructions or, as we explored earlier, Juan Carlos Osorio's systematic patterns and synchronization with the Mexican national team, there is more structure in a typical soccer game than many observers might realize. But the manager in soccer still has less influence on drawing up plays than a coach in the NBA or in the NFL, who can call a time-out and map out the exact choreography of the play he wants to run next. Martínez can't call a time-out. He has to rely on his players following his instructions while responding to challenges and mistakes in the middle of a nonstop game, all the while relying on the chemistry and combination play that have developed over months and years of training sessions together. "You need to have a direction on how we're going to defend and a direction on how we're going to score goals," Martínez explains. "And then it's just trying to be very good in what we normally are as a team."

Chelsea-Everton ends up being an open, frenetic affair, with all six goals scored in the second half. Everton builds a 2–0 lead at Stamford Bridge on a John Terry own goal in the 50th minute (on a cross from Leighton Baines, who got behind Ivanović on the left side) and Mirallas's 56th-minute strike, in which he finds space centrally at the top of the box, spins, and rifles a shot inside the right post that no goalkeeper could save. (It's worth noting that Everton's two most dangerous goal threats to Chelsea—Mirallas and Lukaku—now play for Martínez with Belgium.) But Chelsea strikes back immediately. In the 66th minute, an unpressured Fàbregas lofts a longball to Diego Costa, who takes advantage of a miscommunication by Howard and defender Phil Jagielka to make it 2–1 Everton. Two minutes later, Fàbregas slices through Chelsea's back line and hits a deflected shot past an unlucky Howard for a 2–2 tie.

Stamford Bridge is rocking, and the emotional swings among the Everton and Chelsea fans over the 15-minute stretch are epic. It is becoming one of the great games of the season in the Premier League. At this point, Martínez can most clearly influence the game through his three allowed substitutions. He started thinking about his possible subs long before the game started. "There is no one game in the world where you put a lineup on the field and everyone is 100 percent," he says. "Impossible. That's how football is. It's a contact sport. So you always need to be aware of players that might not be able to finish the 90 minutes."

Martínez says he takes three things into account when deliberating over substitutions: How can you become stronger defensively? How can you open up the opposition better with a tactical switch? And how aware are you of the players who weren't at 100 percent physically leading up to the game? He says he takes additional notice of players who are being asked to do more physically demanding tasks during a game. In this game, that player would be Mirallas, who has been penetrating from a wide position the entire game. Yet Martínez cautions that he never makes hard-and-fast decisions before a game about removing a certain player at a certain minute mark. "Kevin's demands are huge, so after 60 minutes he needs to be assessed, because maybe he won't be able to do that for 90 minutes," Martínez says. "That day he was still fresh, after 70 minutes, when I spoke with him. You look at his physical stats, which were some of the highest in the Premier League. You can't just say, 'No, because it's so demanding, at 60 minutes I'm taking him off.' Well, he was the best player and scored a goal, so why would you take him off? You would be wrong to do that. So what you need to be aware of are two or three areas of concern, and then just tactically bearing in mind if you're finding it difficult to score a goal or to keep a clean sheet. As the game develops, you need to use the substitutions accordingly."

In this game, Martinez's hand is forced by circumstances. Right back Bryan Oviedo suffers an injury and is carried off on a stretcher in the 70th minute. Martínez makes his first substitution, bringing on Ramiro Funes Mori, who goes to centerback while John Stones shifts from centerback to right back. The game settles down from the full-throttle action that produced the four goals in 15 minutes. In the 80th minute, Martínez makes his final two substitutions, introducing midfielders Steven Pienaar and Gerard Deulofeu for Ross Barkley and Aaron Lennon. He's pushing for the go-ahead goal. And wouldn't you know it? The goal comes. In the 90th minute, Mirallas—after creating yet another numerical advantage with Zouma—wins a corner kick. One of Martínez's subs, Deulofeu, whips in a gorgeous cross to the far post, where another sub, Funes Mori, volleys it past Courtois into the goal. 3–2. The Everton players celebrate with their fans in the away supporters' end. Martínez claps his hands and pumps a fist in the air.

But there are *eight* minutes of stoppage time. In the eighth and final minute, Chelsea booms the ball downfield for one last opportunity, and Terry runs onto the ball in the box and scores the last-second equalizer. He's a yard offside, replays show, but the referee doesn't wave off the goal. Even two weeks later, Martínez can't help but shake his head over what can only be seen as two points lost. "At 65 minutes it was the perfect performance," he says. "We were 2–0 up away from home, had a real comfortable lead. Then all of a sudden we made a mistake on one goal. That goal emotionally got the momentum for the home team, and two or three individuals had a big impact on the game. We conceded another one, and it was getting away from us. Then we were able to settle down and get back into competing again. That happens in games. We regained control and scored what should have been the winner in the 90th minute, and then in the 98th minute they allow the goal that should have been offside.

A piece of quality or a bad decision from a referee can change a game. But in general it was a strong performance. We were the better team."

In the final analysis, Martínez's pregame instructions had a net positive impact. Tasked with penetrating the space behind Ivanović and creating chances on goal, Mirallas performed his duties to near perfection, scored a goal, and won the corner that led to Everton's third goal. Then, too, it was two Martínez substitutes, Deulofeu and Funes Mori, who connected on Everton's third goal.

On the other end, Martínez's defensive instruction to defend Willian 2-on-1 had mixed results. Willian did manage some penetrating runs, despite the physical defending he encountered, but he wasn't directly involved in any of Chelsea's goals. The main problem was the knock-on effect from shifting a midfielder over to defend Willian: That left open space in the middle for Fàbregas, who scored once and had zero defensive pressure on him when he delivered his assist to Costa. And, as we learned earlier from Vincent Kompany, putting zero defensive pressure on a talented passer will lead to serious breakdowns in the Premier League.

The 3–3 scoreline is also emblematic of Everton's unusual 2015–16 season, in which one of the league's most fearsome attacks, led by Lukaku, is often let down by defensive lapses. By the time Martínez and I speak a couple weeks after that game, Everton is in 12th place in the league, but it's the only team in that section of the table that has a positive goal difference (plus-6). "For the quality that we have in order to score goals, we concede too many goals," says Martínez. "The reason is not a defensive problem. If you want to use data, it will tell you that our defensive record at home is contrasting to the defensive record away. Now, we don't play any differently. We don't use any different players. But at the moment there is something where we get more punished in our home performances in the way that we defend our goal than we do away from home. The plus-6 [goal difference] tells you that our goal-scoring threat as a team is at the highest level. We shouldn't belong where we are in the table, and we have to improve a few aspects in order to challenge for what this team is building toward."

Martínez is in a strange position in the spring of 2016. His team has scored more goals from open play than any other team in the Premier League. It's an attacking machine. But no matter how you look at it, there *is* a defensive problem. Nor is Martínez naive. He knows he is fighting for his job, due to the high-pressure need for instant results in the Premier League. And yet, as an English-style manager, he's trying to plan for the long term, too. When Martínez talks about what Everton is building toward, he's referring to this season, of course, but also to the coming years. That means giving promising young players opportunities, even if they screw up at times. (John Stones, the young centerback with exceptional skills on the ball, was a prime example in 2015–16, not long before he was sold to Manchester City for £47.5 million, or $62.3 million.) And that means having a keen sense of the modern market for players.

Rare among former players and managers, Martínez has a master's degree in business administration. He pushed Everton chairman Bill Kenwright to spend a club-record £28 million ($47.4 million) transfer fee on Lukaku in 2014 because he was convinced it made sense in the short term (to give Everton an elite centerforward) and in the long term (considering the 21-year-old

Lukaku's huge potential resale value). Ultimately, Everton will sell Lukaku to Manchester United in 2017 for £75 million ($96.7 million). "You need to understand the business side of a football club," Martínez says, "but there are two separate aspects. One is managing the direction of your project, and another one is managing the day-to-day to win a game at the weekend."

In the modern game, though, when fans can pile on the pressure through Twitter and the sack is always just a few losses away for any club manager, the traditional English-style manager role—combining responsibilities for the short *and* long terms—may not be viable much longer. (That's why we're taking a close look at the Continental-style director-of-football role in the next chapter.) Martínez will be fired three months after we watch that memorable Chelsea-Everton game together. He will receive a healthy buyout and another good gig soon in Belgium. But long before any of that happens, he laments the lack of job security in a position that was originally intended to have much more of it than it does today.

"If you have young players with good potential, they need to be given a clear path to become good players, and you need a manager that's got stability in that respect," he says one day. "I hope we understand that the way football clubs are run, you can't go along with the power of social media and everyone wanting a consequence after a bad result. We need to support the boards and the chairmen to give them stability so they can give a manager a real good period of work. If we do that, I think the managers will be working in an environment where the football clubs will benefit at the end of it. Results are what matter in our business—that's just how it is—but it's important that the manager is allowed to be judged over a certain period of time, rather than just being emotional and reactive. Because the modern way of seeing managers has gone that route, and that could be very expensive for a football club and very damaging in terms of achieving something."

Martínez is surely correct, but it seems almost impossible that the way managers are seen in the modern game will revert to what it once was. Much like the Goalkeepers Union, the unwritten rules that keep goalkeepers from criticizing rival keepers, even in private, the unofficial Managers Fraternity thrives in soccer. You encounter it most often when a manager is under fire and other managers, usually respected ones, weigh in with support and say it would be folly to fire their colleague. It's sort of self-sustaining, though. There's no downside to it, and the unspoken understanding is that the supportive manager might need his own public backing down the line.

The Managers Fraternity likes to point out that, under today's standards, Manchester United would almost certainly have fired Sir Alex Ferguson during his first few up-and-down seasons on the job in the late 1980s. Instead, Ferguson stayed until 2013 and became one of the most legendary managers of all time. But the 1980s seem almost quaint compared to today's game. There is too much money at stake now, especially with the threat of relegation from the Premier League and the financial incentives of qualifying for European competition. The intensity of today's global media coverage also ratchets up the pressure. Bottom line: The game isn't reversing course to the 1980s. Maybe having a head coach *and* a director of football is the better way to go.

● ● ●

IN THE SPRING OF 2016, Roberto Martínez finally took some time off. He had been grinding as a manager for nine seasons, since the age of 33, when he had moved directly from the playing field to the coach's box. Managers rarely have the chance to take sabbaticals. After deciding to leave Barcelona in 2012, Pep Guardiola was so exhausted that he spent a year away from managing in New York City, exploring America with his family and perfecting his English—in addition, it turned out, to learning German for his next job with Bayern Munich. Martínez didn't take an entire year off, but the downtime was still restorative for him. "I had a period to just wind down from the intensity of seven consecutive Premier League seasons," he says. "They are really demanding because you can never switch off. Your mind is always trying to organize things. If it's not buying players, it's selling players. So I had a good period with the family, and then the best possible way that you can have therapy, which is watching football."

For a month that summer, Martínez worked in Paris as an analyst for ESPN's coverage of Euro 2016. It was his fifth major tournament on U.S. television, and he was terrific, as usual, breaking down games with an insight, energy, and attention to detail that are still somewhat rare on American soccer broadcasts. (Most of the full-time soccer analysts on U.S. TV are ex-players, not ex-managers.) It's hard to know which is more likely someday: that Martínez becomes the U.S. men's national team coach or that he moves to the United States and turns into American soccer television's answer to John Madden. Some of the smartest discussion on ESPN during Euro 2016 involved Martínez and Vincent Kompany, the Belgium captain, who was missing the tournament with an injury. "I always had the highest of regards toward Vincent as a leader, as the captain of Manchester City," Martínez says. "But when I worked with him for ESPN I realized how intelligent he was. His thirst for the game and his knowledge of it were very, very impressive. But it would be pushing it if I would have thought I would have the opportunity to be his national team coach. In football you need to expect the unexpected. That's the way you live life in sports. But at that point it was far, far away from my head."

The opportunity to meet with the Belgian federation technical committee about its vacant coaching job came out of nowhere, Martínez says, at the start of August 2016. He met with the Belgians during the day, flew back home that night, and a few hours later got a phone call offering him the job. Belgium wanted his decision quickly. "I always base my decisions on feelings," Martínez says a few months later in Tubize. "Once I met the technical committee, I knew this was a real good opportunity to get to know Belgian football, to try to pass my experience on to coaches in the development phase of young players in Belgium, and to try to work with a generation that I feel has the talent to become an interesting team. I'm delighted it was the right decision. I felt I needed the experience that I have in order to take on a national team, but I'm young enough and healthy enough to travel a lot, to watch a lot of live games of our players. They're in Italy and England and Spain. I'm trying to take it as intensely as I can do it."

One of Martínez's first tasks with Belgium was to build his staff. It's a measure of their success, trust, and loyalty that three of his assistants have worked with Martínez since 2007, following him from Swansea City to Wigan Athletic to Everton and now to Belgium. The Englishman Graeme Jones, his top lieutenant, had a 16-year pro career that included three seasons as a teammate of Mártinez at Wigan from 1996 to 1999. "It's probably the biggest contrast you could have," Martínez says. "I was a technical player, coming from the Spanish school, and he was this physical player from the British game. It's like the opposite poles attracted each other. We complement each other really well, and that allows us to cover a lot of ground. It's very helpful for me to get his view, and we can disagree many times, which allows us to see a bit of a wider picture. And he's very loyal, someone I would take to the moon or to war." Knowing someone on a deeply human level, Martínez argues, is especially important on a coaching staff, not least because it allows you to trust that person when things get tough.

Martínez says he has the same level of faith in the two other assistants who have been with him since Swansea—the Spanish goalkeepers coach Iñaki Bergara and the English fitness coach Richard Evans. But as is the case on many national teams, Martínez retained Belgians who had been on the previous staff. Goalkeepers coach Erwin Lemmens stayed on, in part because Martínez likes having four goalkeepers on his roster and thinks it's better to have two coaches working with them (as he did at Everton). The Belgian medical staff remained in place, too. "It was very important that I had the people I had been working with for 10 seasons," Martínez says. "They've got terrific experience, and I trust them. When you haven't got much time at the international level, you can't spend too much time coaching the coaches or the staff. In the same way, I wanted to have a real good influence from staff members from Belgium, and that's what we've done in many of the departments, including the medical department, which is as good as any I had in the Premier League, if not better in certain areas."

The last member of Martínez's staff is an assistant coach who happens to be one of the world's best strikers of the past three decades: the French World Cup and Champions League winner Thierry Henry. At every club he has managed, Martínez says, he has added a staff member of stature who from "an engagement point of view with the players" has been able to connect with them. He did it at Swansea with Alan Curtis, at Wigan with Graham Barrow, and at Everton with Duncan Ferguson. With Belgium, Martínez wanted an assistant who had played at the international level. Henry had been coaching with the Under-18 team at Arsenal, his former club, but he wanted to step up to the senior level while still being able to work in television for Sky Sports in England, where he can keep close tabs on the league in which most of the Belgian national team players compete.

"He's someone who has been through what the players are going through right now," Martínez says of Henry. "They're a great generation that has a lot of expectations, but they have never won a major tournament. He can influence our players a lot from a mental point of view. He's a young coach with incredible potential and his attention to detail is very impressive. It was the perfect fit for the perfect time. Like anything in life, it needs to be right and it felt right." When the players are with the national team during FIFA windows, the entire staff is with the squad. But when the players are with their clubs, the head coach and his assistants are more spread out. Martínez and Jones live full time in Brussels, working from the federation headquarters while monitoring players inside and outside Belgium. Evans, the fitness coach, lives in England, where he visits his counterparts at the Premier League clubs to be on top of the fitness levels for most of the Belgian players. "On the computer we can be linked at any time," says Martínez, "so it works really well."

The website for the Belgian soccer federation lists Martínez's position as *coach*, not *manager*, and that's an accurate reflection of his job description. Martínez may indeed want to work with other Belgian coaches and bring his ideas to the country's youth development programs, but he is being measured on one standard: the performance of the senior national team in the short term. His charge is to compete to win the tournament in Russia. But coaching a national team is nothing like coaching a club team, and Martínez has had to adjust to the rhythms and limitations of his new job. The World Cup remains the biggest sporting event on earth, but in the modern game, club soccer has grown to be more important than international soccer, with the exception of marquee events like the World Cup, the European Championship, and the Copa América.

In some ways, Martínez's job as a national team coach is less complicated than it was at the club level. "You don't have to buy players, and you don't have to sell players," he says by way of explanation. "You don't have to worry about keeping players stimulated at your club, and you don't have to worry about losing players that are important to the group. You can be open-minded about bringing new players into the setup if they qualify to represent the nation. And you know for a fact that the players want to represent their nation and want to play in the team. So that's a very different rule."

"The next change is your time with the players," he continues. "The contact time that you have with the players is very much reduced, and you have to prioritize everything that you want to work on. At club level you've got 60 sessions when you start pre-season to prepare for the first game. When you come into the international scene, you've got 4 sessions to prepare for your first game. That's something that I'm still working on now, but I'm trying to get used to learning about the players when they are away from here. But then when you come together and work, I would say that the intensity is even higher because you live with the players 24 hours a day, and the intensity and the meaning of the games is even bigger [than at club level]." While the overall talent level on Belgium's national team is far higher than that of any club team Martínez has coached, the chemistry on the field is usually lower on a national team than on a club team that trains together nearly year-round.

To reduce conflicts between playing for club and country, FIFA has established international dates over two weeks each in March, June, September, October, and November that allow national teams to play two games per window. (Those don't include Continental tournaments that can take place in June or July.) During FIFA windows, clubs are required to release players to their national teams and domestic leagues are supposed to go quiet. (A few leagues, including Major League Soccer, still schedule some games during international windows.) Martínez has now been on both sides of the club/country divide as a manager, so he understands the need to have a positive relationship with his Belgium players' club managers.

"As a club manager, international football is an intrusion, and it gets in the way of your preparation," he says. "And I'm very aware of that, but in the same way you understand that for the player to fully develop and achieve his own potential, he has to enjoy the pride of representing his nation. That's part of being a footballer. So it's about being aware that the club manager and I can work together. The most important aspect for me is that we share information of what we do in the international camp with the day-to-day at the club. Then the player benefits."

When Martínez isn't with his players, he and his staff monitor them closely. Soon after he took over the Belgium job, Martínez made a list of 55 Belgian players whom he follows regularly at their clubs in a host of different countries. "I'm watching every game on television of every player that is on my list of 55," he says. "And then I'm watching as many games live as I can." It's easier to consume so much soccer, he argues, when he doesn't have to spend time preparing analyses and game plans for two matches a week at the club level. On one day when I interview Martínez in Tubize, he says he's heading later to see the Club Bruges-Oostende Belgian league game live and about to fly to Rome to observe Belgian midfielder Radja Nainggolan play for Roma in person.

What does Martínez look for when he watches his players in the stadium, as opposed to on television? "I'm watching warm-ups, watching the way they act on the touchline, watching the way they celebrate a goal, watching their body language when the team scores and they are not a part of it," he says. "I think you can learn from being at a live game." Some national team managers like to meet for one-on-one discussions with their players after they visit them at their club games, but Martínez is not one of them. Having been on the other side as a club manager, he says, he wouldn't want a national team coach coming in and affecting the preparations of the players for what they're trying to achieve with their clubs.

That said, Martínez wants to be aware of his players' fitness levels at their clubs, and he returns the favor by sharing what he learns when his national team is together. "I've got one staff member that is working directly with the sports scientists department of every football club, so we get all the stats," he says. "Because we need to get to know the players to be efficient and to work in a way that takes into consideration what the players have been doing at club level. I'm trying to do things that I thought were important when I was in a club, and how I wanted the national team coach to look after my players when they were away." When the time comes to put together a player list for call-ups in advance of national team games, Martínez and his staff come up with 23 players and 2 alternates. But he knows he can't control injuries suffered at club level, so, invariably, he says he has to make late changes to the roster. It's all part of the job.

When the Belgian players arrive in the national team camp, Martínez says, he has seen a positive team spirit that goes back to many of the players—Kompany, Vertonghen, Fellaini, Mirallas, Dembélé, and Thomas Vermaelen—participating together as youngsters at the 2008 Olympics. This is no small thing, and it can be affected by the head coach, too. In the final months of Jurgen Klinsmann's tenure as the U.S. men's coach, many of the American players dreaded coming into the national team camp because they questioned Klinsmann's competence at building a plan and communicating that with the team. After Klinsmann was fired following a 4-0 World Cup qualifying loss in Costa Rica (in which several U.S. players appeared to quit) and Bruce Arena replaced him, the U.S. players seemed to enjoy coming into camp again and receiving clear direction from Arena and his staff. That still didn't prevent the U.S. from its shocking failure to qualify for Russia, however.

For Martínez, the biggest challenge in a national team camp is to make the best use of a limited resource: time. "When you're together, it has to be quality time," he says. "Everything you do, from a small session to a recovery session to a tactical session, needs to be done with a purpose and a meaning." Martínez says he doesn't conduct many one-on-one meetings with players, preferring instead to break the team down into small groups to talk about structured concepts and solve any problems that he is seeing in training sessions or games. "Now, more than ever, you're using technology," he says. "Anyone from the new generation is used to using a tablet or a phone, and we use that in camps a lot. They watch clips of good practice and bad practice. I think it's more about finding out what needs to be solved, rather than a structured way of talking with players. They see how they can synchronize things on a football pitch. I think that's important."

Like Mexican national team coach Juan Carlos Osorio, Martínez uses the word *synchronization* to describe what he's trying to achieve with his Belgian team. And, like Osorio, Martínez thinks it should be possible to work on complex tactics in a national team camp, despite the limited amount of time available. For one thing, the players are more talented and (usually) intelligent than those on most club teams, and, as a result, they should be able to grasp new ideas more easily. Besides, it's not like all the national team players are meeting each other for the first time in every camp. "I think you should be able to work tactically in a short period of time," Martínez argues. "I'm not saying the execution is going to be as perfect as it could be at the club level, but then you're going to play against teams that have the same problems. So, in that respect, I want to try things. It can be done."

One difficulty for a new national team coach, however, is the rarity of international games in which there is much at stake. Friendlies, even against top rivals, can devolve into meaningless affairs in which as many as six substitutions are allowed. And even World Cup qualifying in Europe can be a dull slog. Belgium's World Cup 2018 qualifying group included Gibraltar, Cyprus, and Estonia, three teams that won't exactly prepare you to advance beyond the World Cup quarterfinals in 2018. Still, Martínez says he was able to learn valuable information early on in his tenure with Belgium through friendlies that actually meant something. "With friendlies at the international level, you learn very quickly that they can become very much pointless if there is not something to play for," he says. "We played against Spain, which at the time had a new coach in Julen Lopetegui. They had a lot to show, and that was very good for us. Playing Holland away from home, I realized quickly there's never a friendly when you play Holland. Every game is a good opportunity for the players to put their name forward for the final 23."

After Martínez's first game in charge, a 2–0 friendly loss to Spain in which Belgium was played off the field, he once again displayed his old willingness to adapt and make significant changes. He changed Belgium's formation from the back four it had used under Wilmots to a back three. The shift made sense. Belgium is top-heavy with centerbacks, and so lacking in fullbacks that Wilmots had started four centerbacks along the back line. Deploying three elite centerbacks—Kompany, Vertonghen, and Alderweireld—was a smart move that also gave a tactical boost in manpower to the Red Devils' abundant attacking threat. "We need to be flexible tactically," Martínez says. "We changed the system into a back three, which opens the way of playing in a very different manner. It creates 1v1s all over the pitch. It allows players to have a lot more freedom. But in the same way, defensively you need to synchronize a lot more. We needed to change some partnerships and try to develop in those. That has been the biggest variation, just trying to see which players can take bigger roles in the side." More one-on-one situations mean more numerical advantages of the kind that Martínez is always searching for—and nobody can deny that his Belgium team has game-changers who can break down any defenders in the world.

Though Belgium has long been overshadowed in soccer by its neighbor the Netherlands, the Belgians have a long history in the sport and even reached the final of Euro 1980 and the semifinals of the 1986 World Cup. The Red Devils failed to qualify for a major tournament in the 12 years between 2002 and 2014, and yet the groundwork for a new generation of talent was already being laid in the late 1990s. After World Cup 1998, Martínez says, Belgian federation officials began visiting other federations that had been successful in youth development and forged their own plan to point toward a specific playing style. "From that point, many aspects were structured," Martínez says. "Their system was going to be a 4-3-3 trying to produce a good attacking, technical style of football. When that message went through, that affected the clubs in the pro league and the sports schools in the country, and the whole way of developing play-ers was very clear. From that point on, you could see an evo-lution." Martínez argues that the Belgian league has become a reliable incubator of that young talent, much of which possesses the attributes to move on to the English Premier League. When you hear Martínez discuss the diverse skill set of the attacking stars at his disposal with Belgium, you can understand why he wanted the job with the Red Devils. What coach in the world would turn down the opportunity to work with these guys? Just listening to Martínez describe them with his insight and enthusiasm is a treat.

On Romelu Lukaku, the young Manchester United striker who led the Belgian league in scoring at age 16: "He's got the obsession of becoming the best, and I haven't seen that in too many European players. You see it in South American and Central American players, because they've got that focus of coming to Europe and wanting to achieve, to be traveling back home and feel proud. And I haven't seen that obsession as strong as Rom has. Rom, as someone who had the power and the strength to do whatever he wanted at 16 on a football pitch, all of a sudden he found out that he had to learn the game and go through phases and still develop that enormous potential. When I decided to pay the money that we paid at Everton, it was because I believed in the player that he could be, not the player that he was. And when you've got a player with the obsession of becoming the best, you'll never go wrong by supporting that potential. In other players, you can see good potential, but then the drive of the human being is not there, so that potential never flourishes. Rom, for me, can be anything that he wants to. He can be the perfect number nine: a number nine that holds the ball up, who's good with his back to the goal. He's someone who can run with the ball, who can run in behind, and he's got the power and the pace to get away from defenders. And he's a finisher. It's a joy to see him grow, because once he was a very young boy in football terms, and now he's becoming a man. And I'm hoping that over the next two years I can see the finished article."

On Eden Hazard, the dynamic winger and former Premier League player of the year with Chelsea: "When you suffer Eden as an opposing manager, you see the enormous, stylish talent that he has. He can turn right and left, and he's got such a strong lower body. That is quite refreshing, to see an attacking player that encourages contact. He never wants to go down or buy a free kick. He's someone who can hold a challenge and then use that enormous talent in the 1v1 situation. What really surprised me is the leadership capacity that he has, as someone who leads others through pure respect and the love that he has for the game. And that's really unique to see in an attacking player. When Eden is in full flow on a football pitch, you're not going to see many players around the world that have got that threat, that something could happen out of nothing."

On Kevin De Bruyne, the game-breaking attacking midfielder for Manchester City: "Kevin is such an intelligent footballer. His technical ability is special, but I think it's more the capacity for him to understand football and footballing concepts. When you see him on the pitch, it's always the perfect pass, always the right decision, always the execution of what he tries to do that is impressive. He's had a big challenge at Manchester City when a new manager comes with such clear ideas like Pep Guardiola. And straight away he picks those up. His football intelligence is quite remarkable, and when you've got players like that, it's very easy to fit into a team. But it's important that we fit all these players with a very specific role within the side. We can't become just players that are trying to do the same thing. What's important is that each of these players, they've got an outstanding attribute, and we have to find a way to use those outstanding attributes together in the same team, which is just not easy."

De Bruyne, Hazard, and Lukaku are household names in any soccer-watching household around the world, and yet part of Martínez's satisfaction in the Belgium job has come from learning more about players who haven't been stars in the Premier League. Guys like Axel Witsel, the Chinese-based two-way midfielder who Martínez says gives Belgium a needed balance; or Youri Tielemans, the rising 20-year-old midfielder whom Martínez gave his debut to before Tielemans moved to Monaco from Anderlecht in the summer of 2017; or Nacer Chadli, the winger who has had a modest Premier League career but has been reliable as a national team starter under Martínez. "We've got a really, really strong squad, so I think you could enjoy being in that dressing room," Martínez says. "If you're a player, you're going to be challenged from the first second because the level is so high. And, as a coach, it's interesting to see how quickly these players understand concepts and can put them into practice."

One day, I come right out and ask Martínez: Does this Belgium team have enough talent to win the World Cup? He pauses in thought for a moment. Deep down he knows the answer is yes, and his answer indicates that without him having to say so. "Does the most talented team always win?" he asks. "Because the answer is no. Portugal won the Euro. We've got exceptional talent, and I think that represents what Belgium is, a nation that's based on creativity, on going forward, on diversity, but always trying to score goals. The talent is there. Now we need to learn how to be a winning team. Talent on its own, especially when you're not working together for 10 months, is not enough to win a major tournament. We've never had the direction before."

Martínez compares Belgium to France before it won World Cup 1998 and Spain before it won Euro 2008—teams that long had the talent to raise a major trophy but needed to blast through a mental barrier before doing so. Once they did, more than one title—and greatness—followed in their path.

To Martínez, finding success with Belgium is not about putting his 11 most talented players on the field together. It's about finding the right balance, about having the ingredients to compete for 90 minutes against teams—such as Greece in World Cup qualifying—that are happy to sit back and let you spin your wheels to break them down. The Belgian players are no different from Christian Pulisic, who has to remind himself not to get too frustrated when he tries every trick in his repertoire and can't quite find the right combination on some days. How resilient are you going to be? "The mentality is the biggest area we have to improve," Martínez says. "When you speak with people like [former German star] Michael Ballack, for them it's normal: You go to the national team and you win. That's what you do. Over 90 minutes, sometimes you have moments where it's not about playing well, but it's about controlling those moments. We need to work on the psychology and the mental aspect of being a team—in terms of getting clarity in the way we want to play, being flexible enough in how we play and having enough opportunity to mix the talent together. We need the right mentality to get through the difficult moments of a game."

For his part, Martínez's own mental approach with Belgium is not to try to relitigate the past from Everton. He says he feels no specific personal need to show that his team can defend well in addition to scoring goals. There is no, shall we say, defensiveness about the topic. He says his main desire is to fulfill the giant hopes of Belgians, families from around the country who registered their displeasure over the Euro 2016 fiasco by whistling at their own team in Martínez's first game. "I'll never change the way I believe the game should be played, and I'll always work hard to perfect that style," Martínez says. "As a coach, or as a manager, it's your choice how you want to play the game. My aspiration of taking this job is to try and fulfill the potential of this group and the expectations of the Belgian public. There have only been 20 World Cups, and in the grand scheme that's a small number. To be a part of that would be an amazing feeling. That's what the hard work is for."

He will likely return to club coaching at some point. Martínez is too young and has too much energy to spend 10 months of the year without his players. But the chance to coach a collective with so much possibility is rare. Martínez has an opportunity to make history with Belgium, to take a team that's worse than the sum of its parts and turn that around completely. On such accomplishments managerial careers are made.

6

THE DIRECTOR OF FOOTBALL

Michael Zorc's Formula One Ford Mustang

WHAT DO YOU DO?

It's one of the most common questions that people ask upon meeting someone anywhere in the world. But even if you know that Michael Zorc is Borussia Dortmund's sporting director, even if you know that he's widely regarded as the finest director of football in European soccer, even if you know that Arsenal tried (and failed) to hire him away from Dortmund in 2017, you find yourself wanting to end any confusion. After all, not even the global soccer community can agree on the job title for one of the most important positions in the modern game—that is, if you choose to have one at all. Sporting director, director of football, technical director, general manager—all those terms can be used to characterize what Zorc does in his work.

Which is . . . what, exactly?

What do you do?

Facing the most basic of inquiries, Zorc can't help but laugh. "It is a simple question," he says during one of our interviews at Dortmund's business headquarters, not far from Signal Iduna Park, "but not simple to describe."

Born and bred in Dortmund, a small working-class German city in what used to be coal country, Zorc played his entire career as a central midfielder with Borussia Dortmund from 1981 to 1998. Though he had only seven caps for the German national team, Zorc was a rock for BVB, making a club-record 463 Bundesliga appearances, wearing the captain's armband, and winning two Bundesliga titles and the 1996–97 UEFA Champions League trophy. Zorc was a solid player and respected as a leader. And even though he scored only rarely in the run of play, he piled up the goals as an expert in taking penalty kicks. In the sport's crucible of maximum pressure, Zorc didn't blink.

It's a skill that he has brought to the negotiating table, the boardroom, and the training fields as a Dortmund executive since 1998, becoming the sporting director in 2005. "I am responsible for the whole football department," he says in English, "for recruiting the squad for Borussia Dortmund—the players and sometimes the coach as well—and taking care of the whole group and organizing everything around the games. I'm also responsible for the philosophy from the first team to the youth teams, discussing it with the coach, and the youth teams have to follow how the first team is playing. Our philosophy is linked to our region, a working-class region. So it has to be daring, it has to be attacking. The fans don't like it when the team plays like chess on the field. That's a very important point. More specific to the professional team, I am responsible for, let's say, human resources—for buying players, selling players, prolonging contracts, and so on. I'm on top of the scouting department and taking care of players, so that they have someone they can talk to besides the coach. So I am always with the team during the matches. I attend all the training sessions. Not for the whole time, but maybe before or after training I will have lunch or dinner with the team, so that you are there, so they know somebody from the club is taking care."

In most traditional English-style clubs, the chain of command is different. At the top is ownership. Usually there is a board with a chairperson, who hires the manager, who's in charge of the soccer strategy over the short to long terms. At Arsenal, for example, the dominant figure in every soccer decision for years has been manager Arsène Wenger, although the club appears to be moving toward a change in structure that would institute a director of football to spread responsibilities more evenly.

Most German and Continental clubs have an alternative chain of command. By statute, the majority "owners" are the dues-paying members of the clubs. Borussia Dortmund is run by CEO Hans-Joachim Watzke, who has been in charge since 2005, with Zorc on top of the soccer side. Who is Zorc's boss? "Mr. Watzke," he says with a smile. "He can fire me. It's very easy. But we are working now together for more than a decade. It's a very trusting relationship between us." Who hires the head coach? "It's me and Mr. Watzke," Zorc says. "That's very helpful in this club, that there's just Mr. Watzke and me who decide these important things." And who is the head coach's boss? "First case, me," Zorc says. "And then, on top of this, our CEO."

Most clubs that have a sporting director or director of football use the term *head coach* or *trainer*, instead of *manager*, to describe the person in charge of the first team. "The coach," says

Zorc, "is responsible for the tactics, for how we play, and to choose the players for each game." Player transfers—incoming and outgoing—are Zorc's domain, though the CEO and the head coach usually play roles as well. "The CEO is responsible for the budget you can handle," Zorc says. "Normally in recent years, we discuss [transfers] with the CEO and me and then the coach at the end, when it's about a big transfer."

Zorc cuts the imposing figure of a former elite professional athlete. He's more stylish than most soccer executives, with a taste for Hugo Boss sweaters, cashmere scarves, and the occasional tailored suit, though he doesn't look out of place in black-and-yellow Dortmund training gear. Known for his long, flowing hair during his playing days, he now wears it a bit shorter, often slicked back. He is undeniably handsome, a Teutonic version of Alec Baldwin.

If it sounds like Zorc has more power at Borussia Dortmund than the head coach, that's because he does. In the 2016–17 season, coach Thomas Tuchel guided BVB to the Champions League quarterfinals and third place in the Bundesliga (enough to qualify for Champions League again), in addition to winning the German Cup knockout tournament. But three days after raising that trophy in Berlin, Tuchel was out of a job. There were many reasons for Tuchel's departure, but the genesis of the split was friction between Tuchel and Dortmund's renowned chief scout, Sven Mislintat, over transfer targets. And Mislintat, who worked for Dortmund from 1998 until he left for Arsenal in 2017, reported to Zorc. "He's in my department, not the coach's," Zorc says. "Our scouts report to the chief scout, and I speak to Sven every day." BVB's head coach may be on global television all the time, but there's no doubt who's in charge at the club.

"Michael Zorc stands for Borussia Dortmund like no one else," Watzke said upon announcing Zorc's five-year contract extension through 2019, noting that Zorc has been with the club since 1978 (when he joined its youth ranks).

Explaining the chain of command and what Zorc does allows you to understand why he's so good at his job. In the modern game, money matters. In their book *Soccernomics*, Simon Kuper and Stefan Szymanski calculated that 92 percent of the differences in English soccer clubs' league position can be explained by a club's relative salary bill. Borussia Dortmund is by no means poor—remember, it has the highest average attendance of any club in the world—but BVB's annual revenues are nowhere near those of the clubs it aspires to compete against, whether it's German nemesis Bayern Munich or megawealthy Champions League rivals like Real Madrid, Barcelona, Manchester United, Paris Saint-Germain, and Manchester City.

"It's a big challenge, one that you normally can't win very often," says Zorc, "because we are talking about professional football, and we have to talk about money. Our aim is always to be at the top of Germany, or at least behind Bayern Munich, and, if you transfer it to Europe, we have to reach the quarterfinals of Champions League, which means that you are among the best eight clubs in Europe. But the problem we are facing, especially compared to Bayern Munich and the big guys from England and Spain, and now from PSG, is revenue. All these clubs have [annual] revenues of more than €500 million [$588 million]. We've hit €370 million, but that was including transfers, so our basic revenue is about €300 million. So that means we are lacking €200 million of revenue, which means €100 million as a budget for the team. That's our challenge. If this was Formula One, they're driving a Ferrari, and we're driving, I don't know, a Ford Mustang."

The obstacle facing Zorc—trying to compete with teams that have far higher revenues—is the same one tackled by Oakland Athletics general manager Billy Beane in Michael Lewis's classic book *Moneyball*. Zorc's response hasn't been exactly like Beane's; European soccer doesn't employ a draft system to acquire prospects the way baseball does, and while Zorc says he and his staff use some Beane-style data metrics to identify transfer targets, they also rely heavily on their traditional scouting system. (More on that later.) Zorc knows better than anyone that Dortmund has to focus on finding *value* for talent, recognizing that its players are assets and an important part of the club's revenue equation. "We have to have a different approach to compete," he says. "We have to be more creative. We have to be quicker in taking decisions and finding players. And we have to find *different* players. We can't go on the market like Real Madrid and just buy anyone we want. We are trying to find players who have not reached the highest level."

No director of football in Europe has done better than Zorc when it comes to identifying young talent, buying at a low price, and selling for a high price—all while keeping Dortmund in a position to spend most of the past decade competing to win European soccer's most prestigious club trophies. The pricing on transfer fees is influenced by a number of variables. How good is the player right now? And how much potential does he have for the future? The more time a player has left on his current contract, the higher his price will be. And the younger the player, the higher his potential resale value will be a few years down the line. Once a player hits age 29 or 30, his transfer price usually declines because his resale value in his 30s will be much lower.

Broadly speaking, the consummation of a player transfer requires two separate negotiations—one between the selling club and the buying club on the transfer fee, and the other between the buying club and the player on a new contract. (There will usually also be a negotiation between the buying club and the agents about the agents' fees.) Unlike in American pro sports leagues, where a player can almost always be traded without his approval, a player transfer in soccer requires the player to *agree* to make the move and then to negotiate a salary with his new team. If a player completes his contract with a team, he is a free agent and can move to a new club on a free transfer.

In 2010, Zorc took Mislintat's recommendation and paid €4.8 million for a relatively unknown 21-year-old Polish striker named Robert Lewandowski, who had led the Polish third, second, and first divisions in scoring. Lewandowski went on to become one of the world's best centerforwards—he famously scored four goals against Real Madrid on Dortmund's run to the 2013 Champions League final—and in 2018 had a market value of €80 million with Bayern Munich. (BVB could have sold Lewandowski to Bayern a year earlier for big money, but decided to get one more season out of him and let him play out his contract.) Also in 2010, Zorc signed midfielder Shinji Kagawa for a paltry €350,000 from a Japanese club (Cerezo Osaka) that few soccer people had even heard of. Kagawa became the Bundesliga player of the year before being sold to Manchester United in 2012 for €16 million. (He returned to Dortmund two years later.)

Zorc and Mislintat developed a reputation for spotting and signing talent from places that aren't traditional strongholds, and not just Japan and Poland. American Christian Pulisic, who joined Dortmund's youth academy for free as a 15-year-old in 2015, quickly turned into one of the best prospects in Europe. Zorc has also paid remarkably low prices for players from modest French clubs, including striker Pierre-Emerick Aubameyang (€13 million from Saint-Étienne), winger Ousmane Dembéle (€15 million from Rennes) and fullback Raphaël Guerreiro (€12 million from Lorient). Even inside Germany, Zorc has found diamonds in the rough, from defender Mats Hummels (bought for €4.2 million, sold for €35 million back to Bayern Munich) to midfielder Ilkay Gündoğan (bought for €5.5 million, sold for €27 million to Manchester City) to midfielder Julian Weigl (bought for €2.5 million and now worth 10 times as much). Not every signing has worked out—see Ciro Immobile and Julian Schieber—but Zorc's success rate is remarkable compared to his competition.

PLAYER	BOUGHT FOR	SOLD FOR	2018 VALUE
Ousmane Dembélé	€15 million (2016)	€105 million (2017)&	€105 million
Robert Lewandowski	€4.8 million (2010)	Free (2014)^	€80 million
Pierre-Emerick Aubameyang	€13 million (2013)	€63.8 million (2018)	€63.8 million
Christian Pulisic	Free (2015)#		€45 million
Mats Hummels	€4.2 million (2009)	€35 million (2016)	€40 million
Marco Reus	€17.1 million (2012)		€35 million
Henrikh Mkhitaryan	€27.5 million (2013)	€42 million (2016)	€35 million

PLAYER	BOUGHT FOR	SOLD FOR	2018 VALUE
Ivan Perišić	€5.5 million (2011)	€8 million (2013)	€35 million
Ilkay Gündoğan	€5.5 million (2011)	€27 million (2016)	€30 million
Sokratis	€9.9 million (2013)		€28 million
Julian Weigl	€2.5 million (2015)		€25 million
Andriy Yarmolenko	€25 million (2017)		€22.5 million
Ciro Immobile	€18.5 million (2014)	€11 million (2016)	€22.5 million
Maximilian Philipp	€18 million (2017)		€20 million
Raphaël Guerreiro	€12 million (2016)		€20 million
André Schürrle	€30 million (2016)		€20 million
Mario Götze	Free (2001)#	€37 million (2013)%	€20 million
Ömer Toprak	€10.8 million (2017)		€16 million
Matthias Ginter	€10 million (2014)	€17 million (2017)	€15 million
Gonzalo Castro	€11 million (2015)	€10.5 million (2018)	€10.5 million
Marc Bartra	€8 million (2016)		€15 million
Mahmoud Dahoud	€10.8 million (2017)		€13.5 million
Shinji Kagawa	€0.35 million (2010)	€16 million (2012)*	€13 million
Sven Bender	€1.5 million (2009)	€12.5 million (2017)	€11 million

PLAYER	BOUGHT FOR	SOLD FOR	2018 VALUE
Roman Bürki	€3.5 million (2015)		€9 million
Marcel Schmelzer	Free (2005)		€9 million
Mikel Merino	€3.75 million (2016)	€7 million (2017)	€7 million
Jeremy Toljan	€5 million (2017)		€6 million
Alexander Isak	€8.6 million (2017)		€5.4 million
Nuri Şahin	Free (2001)#	€10 million (2011)**	€5 million
Adrián Ramos	€9.7 million (2014)	€12 million (2017)	€5 million
Jadon Sancho	€6.3 million (2017)		€5 million
Łukasz Piszczek	Free (2010)		€5 million
Neven Subotić	€4.5 million (2008)	Free (2018)	€5 million
Emre Mor	€9.75 million (2016)	€13 million (2017)	€4.5 million
Sebastian Rode	€12 million (2016)		€4.5 million
Erik Durm	Free (2012)		€3.5 million
Felix Passlack	Free (2012)#		€3 million
Jakub Blaszczykowski	€3.1 million (2007)	€5 million (2016)	€2.7 million
Dan-Axel Zagadou	Free (2017)		€2.5 million
Julian Schieber	€5.5 million (2012)	€2.5 million (2014)	€2 million

PLAYER	BOUGHT FOR	SOLD FOR	2018 VALUE
Lucas Barrios	€4.2 million (2009)	€8.5 million (2012)	€1.75 million
Steven Pienaar	Free (2006)	€2.75 million (2008)	€1 million
Nelson Valdez	€4.7 million (2006)	€3.5 million (2010)	€0.65 million
Mladen Petrić	€3.5 million (2007)	€7.3 million (2008)	N/A
David Odonkor	Free (2002)#	€6.5 million (2006)	N/A
Ebi Smolarek	€0.75 million (2005)	€4.5 million (2007)	N/A
Alexander Frei	€4.1 million (2006)	€4.25 million (2009)	N/A
Mohamed Zidan	€2.8 million (2008)	€0.4 million (2012)	N/A

SOURCE: TRANSFERMARKT.COM

  &   25% of Dembélé's sale to Barcelona went to his previous French club, Rennes.
  #   Borussia Dortmund youth academy product.
  *   Kagawa returned to Borussia Dortmund in 2014 for an €8 million transfer fee.
  ^   Dortmund decided to let Lewandowski play out his contract.
  ** Şahin returned to Borussia Dortmund in 2014 for a €7 million transfer fee.
  %   Götze returned to Borussia Dortmund in 2016 for a €22 million transfer fee.

In fact, elite directors of football are even rarer in the modern game than world-class managers and coaches. Perhaps that's because there's so little understanding of what a director of football does. Or maybe it's just extremely difficult to perform the job well. Other directors of football who have gained sterling reputations are Giuseppe Marotta (Juventus), Ralf Rangnick (RB Leipzig), Walter Sabatini (Inter Milan), and Marcel Brands (PSV Eindhoven). But probably the most lionized sporting director other than Zorc is Spaniard Ramón Rodríguez Verdejo, better known as Monchi, who spent 17 years as the director of football at Sevilla and gave a launchpad to such players as Sergio Ramos, Dani Alves, Jesús Navas, and Ivan Rakitić. "Monchi is absolutely outstanding," says Zorc. "He did a tremendous job for Sevilla. It's a different situation at Sevilla, I think, because nobody really expected him and Sevilla to fight against Barcelona and Real Madrid. For him it was about qualifying for Champions League, winning the Europa League, and buying players low and selling high. For us, it's more about reaching sporting goals. The difference is we have 80,000 people in our stadium who don't care about our bank account. They want the players to win on the field."

In 2017, Monchi moved from Sevilla to Roma, where the expectations of winning Italian league titles and going deep into Champions League will be much higher—which is to say, more like they are at Dortmund. Since Zorc took on the title of BVB sporting director in 2005, Dortmund has won two Bundesliga titles (finishing runner-up three times) and two German Cup titles, in addition to reaching the Champions League quarterfinals three times and the final once. Zorc's job isn't just to buy low and sell high. Every season he has to keep Dortmund in the conversation among the very best in Europe. Every season he has to build another souped-up, jerry-rigged, Formula One Ford Mustang.

IF YOU WERE WRITING A modern history of Borussia Dortmund, the pivotal year would not be any of those in which BVB won the Champions League or the Bundesliga or the German

Cup. It would be 2005, when years of poor decisions on the budget side finally caught up with one of Germany's most famous clubs. Why, even Bayern Munich had to give Dortmund an emergency loan just to help keep BVB afloat. "We nearly went bankrupt in 2005," says Zorc of the year that Watzke became the CEO and started to clean things up. "Before this, we always bought expensive players and paid the highest salaries, even compared to Bayern Munich in the 1990s, when we won the Champions League. So we had to identify a new strategy."

Back in the 1990s, Zorc was one of the few Dortmund players who *wasn't* cashing in big on the club's free spending. ("Unfortunately, it was only for the foreign players," he cracks.) But by the time he took on the sporting director title in 2005, Zorc resolved to maximize value in a few different ways. One was by investing in Dortmund's youth academy, which has produced such players as Mario Götze, Nuri Şahin, Felix Passlack, and Christian Pulisic. Another was by identifying talented players (including young prospects) who may have been overlooked, both in Germany and in countries where Dortmund's big Champions League rivals might not have been looking very closely.

Zorc's process of developing a strategy has been long and is ongoing, but he can draw a through-line of Dortmund's top strikers over the years, all of whom play for non–blue blood national teams and were purchased from clubs that are (in terms of European powerhouses) off the beaten track. In 2006, Zorc bought Alexander Frei, a 27-year-old Swiss striker, from France's Rennes for €4.1 million. Three years later came Lucas Barrios, a 24-year-old Paraguayan centerforward, from Chile's Colo-Colo for €4.2 million. In 2010, Zorc signed the 21-year-old Lewandowski from Poland's Lech Poznan for €4.8 million, and three years later came Aubameyang, a 24-year-old striker for Gabon from France's Saint-Étienne for €13 million. All four strikers performed at a high level for Dortmund, and all four—except Lewandowski, who played out his entire contract—were sold for more than Zorc's purchase price.

Remarkably, Lewandowski had been rejected by Sporting Gijón, a Spanish top-flight bottom feeder, not long before Dortmund signed him. But Zorc and Mislintat liked what they saw in the young Pole. "He's now one of the best strikers in the world," Zorc says. "It's about statistics, especially when it comes to strikers. I like strikers who score; everybody does. But there are some strikers who score for one year and then you don't see them again. And he, as a young player, had a very good track record being the best striker in Poland in the third division, then in the second division, and then again in the first division. That's what I like, the graduation of a player. Then you know there's a high probability that he will score in your club as well."

One of the most crucial moments in the process came in May 2008, when Zorc and Watzke hired Jürgen Klopp, a young, wildly energetic head coach who had made a coaching name for himself in Germany at Mainz. Klopp's relentless, high-pressing style was a hit with Dortmund fans, and he possessed a quality— his willingness to engage with young players and make them better—that fit Zorc's strategy perfectly. With Klopp's arrival, BVB started buying more prospects who were in their late teens and early 20s. "This happened especially after signing Klopp," Zorc says. "We started to find these promising players and to develop them. We always like to have coaches who like to work with young players. That's very important for us as a philosophy."

Some of those young players arrived ready to play in the

Bundesliga, but not all of them did. The 80,000 fans who fill Dortmund's stadium wanted their team to win, and Zorc knew he couldn't do that just by signing youngsters. "I like to buy prospective players, but with only prospective players you don't win the title at the end," he says. "So we had a two-column strategy." Klopp's Dortmund became a mix of young talent and players with more experience, all united behind a dynamic playing style that required full commitment from everyone. And BVB won: Bundesliga titles in 2010–11 and 2011–12, followed by an inspiring run to the 2012–13 Champions League final before losing to Bayern Munich. Klopp's seven-year Dortmund coaching tenure ended in 2015 after an outlier seventh-place Bundesliga finish—he would eventually take over at Liverpool—but Zorc continued his strategy of hiring coaches who develop promising talent: first Tuchel in 2015 and then Peter Bosz, a Dutchman who had led a remarkably young Ajax squad to the 2016–17 Europa League final. Bosz was a spectacular flameout, however, presiding over a team that struggled mightily in the defense, and he was fired in December 2017.

Over the years, Dortmund developed a reputation as a club that not only competed to win trophies and displayed an exciting brand of soccer, but it also provided playing opportunities to top prospects at a high level and ultimately sold several of them to the wealthiest clubs in the world. Whether it was Şahin to Real Madrid in 2011, Kagawa to Manchester United in 2012, or Gündoğan to Manchester City in 2016, Dortmund became known as one of the best stepping-stones in European soccer—a place where, unlike at Real Madrid or Chelsea, a prospect could actually get playing time instead of being stuck on the bench or sent out on loan. In time, some top prospects started *turn-*

ing down more lucrative offers from the biggest clubs in favor of what would be better for their career (for a few years, at least) at Borussia Dortmund.

"One of our most important goals is to find these kinds of players who identify Borussia Dortmund as the step for themselves to become the best players they can be," Zorc says. "They may have more financially attractive offers from the five or six bigger clubs, especially from England. For example, Raphaël Guerreiro: When we bought him, he also had offers from PSG and from Barcelona, but more as a backup in those clubs. He had to face fierce competition there. And here, we like to buy these players at the age of 18 to 23, when their development isn't finished yet."

Like Guerreiro, who had played for Portugal's Euro 2016 champions before joining Dortmund, French winger Ousmane Dembélé was known by every club in Europe in the summer of 2016, when he moved from Rennes at age 19. This was no out-of-nowhere signing by Dortmund like Kagawa or Lewandowski in 2010. ("Even Stevie Wonder could see his talent," Zorc jokes about Dembélé.) But for Dembélé, at least on this career decision, money wasn't everything. "Because of the reputation we have in France, they see the way young players go at Borussia Dortmund," Zorc says. "Before we signed Dembélé, he phoned Aubameyang and asked him, 'How is the club?' And [Aubameyang] convinced him to sign for Borussia Dortmund. He could sign for Real Madrid, Bayern Munich, Barcelona, both [Manchester] clubs, but he chose Borussia Dortmund, at least for his next step. Maybe in the eyes of these very high-ranked players, we are not the last club where they want to be. But we're at least the best step to become one of the best players in football."

In some ways, Zorc and Dortmund have been the beneficiaries of a cautionary tale. In 2014, the hottest prospect in European soccer was a Norwegian 15-year-old midfielder named Martin Ødegaard, whose dribbling and scoring feats in the Norwegian pro league had made him a YouTube legend. "I went there and met his father," Zorc says, "and he said, 'I've been to Barcelona, Milan, Juventus, and Bayern Munich.' He went everywhere. And then he signed for Real Madrid. It was the biggest package for father, son, and club. But, sporting-wise, it wasn't the best idea." After spending two years with Real Madrid's reserve team, Ødegaard went on an 18-month loan to Heerenveen in the Netherlands in 2017.

Dembélé wasn't going to make the same mistake that Ødegaard did. And wouldn't you know it? Right after Dortmund signed Dembélé, BVB drew Real Madrid in its Champions League group. "We won our Champions League group [in 2016–17] ahead of Real Madrid," Zorc says. "If Dembélé had chosen Real Madrid as his club, I don't know that he would have played as many games as he did here." Ultimately, Dortmund got one terrific season out of Dembélé before selling him to Barcelona in August 2017 for €105 million—a full €90 million more than BVB had paid for him just one year earlier.

Zorc won again.

THE GEOGRAPHY OF BVB'S PROPERTIES in the city of Dortmund parallels the organizational flowchart at the club. The training ground and academy—the domain of the head coach, the technical staff, and the players—are located in a quiet neigh-

borhood on the east side of the city. The stadium, Signal Iduna
Park, is in a central section of Dortmund, not far from the glass-
and-steel building on Rheinlanddamm that serves as the club's
business headquarters. This is the domain of the CEO, Watzke;
the promotions, marketing, and events staffs; and the sporting
director, Zorc, as well as the chief scout and the scouts who work
beneath them. The person who divides his time more than any
other at *both* the business office and the training ground is Zorc.

On a rainy afternoon in April, Zorc is in a conference room
at the business office, explaining how he and his scouting staff
identify potential player targets for acquisition. "I don't know if
it's any secret," he says. "It's just doing your homework, being dil-
igent. There are about 10 scouts working here in our office and
another 5 regional scouts who are responsible for their country
or region. That is my whole staff. These days you can't have manpower in every stadium in the world, so it's about the internet
and watching many, many matches with our devices."

Zorc says Dortmund, like most clubs around the world,
uses a data-and-analytics service to provide information about
players and help separate those who might be a good fit for
his club. But to hear him tell the story, Dortmund's success in
the transfer market comes down more than anything to traditional scouting. "We have an old system as well, and we are
giving grades like in school," he explains. "And you go to these
certain characteristics. Football characteristics. Then at the
end you have a summary. It's not a computer system. It's more
about characteristics that are important to us. It depends on
the position. For a central midfielder, it would be good vision of
the game, good in ball possession, playing responsibly, passing
skills. If you take Julian Weigl, in this position he's not allowed

to lose many balls, because then the counterattack is against only your two central defenders."

For most players, Zorc says, he seeks opinions from many scouts on his staff, the better to reach a consensus. That's not always possible, especially with some of Dortmund's employees. "I have one scout, a very old scout," Zorc says. "Because no player is good enough for him, we call him The Destroyer. So if I want a real hard opinion, I send The Destroyer. He's very old-fashioned. A former coach, 74 years old. Sometimes he'll say, I didn't watch the game. When I saw him warming up, I thought, 'He's not a player.'" On other occasions, though, Zorc says it only takes a few minutes watching a special player to realize that he doesn't need a bunch of opinions from his staff. "Fifteen years ago when you saw Tomáš Rosický, or now when you see Dembélé, you know you don't need to send 20 scouts because, hey, that's him," Zorc says. *We have to get him.* Especially for strikers, at a young age they have to have specific, outstanding skills. A player like Dembélé might have 20 mistakes in the whole game, but there are two or three actions in one game when you say, 'We have to get this player.' And that's the difficulty: to identify these kinds of skills. It's difficult to describe them, but it's also about a feeling."

Once Zorc decides he's interested in a player, he says, his staff will do extensive research on the player's history. He will contact the player's agent and find out if any other clubs are interested, in addition to gauging the agent's interest in Dortmund and the length of the player's current contract. "Normally, these days, it's about the agent," Zorc says. "You're not allowed to go directly to the player. The main information is how long is his contract. If you have a player who's signed until 2021, it's worthless to go for him." Now that he has been in his job for so many years, Zorc says he has a good idea of pricing and what will work for Dortmund. After he has decided to pursue a player, Zorc contacts the player's club. If there is interest, a negotiation will commence. Zorc trusts his pricing instincts. "We tried to buy Ömer Toprak from Leverkusen last summer [in 2016], but he was too expensive, and they refused to sell him for our price," Zorc explains. "The price they were asking was too much for me, and then we said no. And now he has a buyout clause [of €10.8 million], and we just paid. It's half the price they were demanding last summer."

Buyout clauses—which obligate a club to sell a player if another club offers to pay a certain fee and the player wants to leave—are a sensitive topic for Dortmund fans. In 2013, BVB lost star forward Mario Götze when archrival Bayern Munich triggered his release clause for €37 million. A Dortmund academy product, Götze was vilified by the club's fans for choosing to leave, though he eventually returned to the team in 2016. Bayern has a history of acquiring Dortmund's best players, including Lewandowski after his contract expired in 2014 and Mats Hummels on a €35 million transfer in 2016, and Zorc would typically prefer for any other club *except* Bayern to poach one of his stars. "I like buyout clauses *in other clubs*," he says with a smile. "None of our players has a buyout clause right now. That was a process achieved by our sporting success, and also by our financial strength we've achieved now. So we say, 'You're playing for Borussia Dortmund in Champions League. In the last seven years we finished at least second in the league four times. You are earning this kind of money. So no buyout clause.' But I like it for players in other clubs. It makes it easy."

✦ ✦ ✦

IN A PERFECT WORLD, ZORC would prefer never to sell any of the players he wants to keep. But contracts only last so long, and a player who's successful at Dortmund may have ambitions to play at an even bigger, wealthier club. Zorc winces whenever Dortmund is described as a "selling club"—"I don't like this, no, no, no," he says, "because we still have our own goals and expectations"—but he acknowledges the reality that if Barcelona wants to pay big money for Dembélé, BVB won't stand in the way. "None of our top players would go to Stoke City. Even if they would pay higher salaries, they would stay here," Zorc says. "But we have to admit that there are, let's say, five or six clubs that are much bigger than Borussia Dortmund. It's about money, it's about the duration of the contract and of the decision not to prolong. We are not a club that likes to sell players, but still we have it in mind when we buy players that at some point in time we may sell them, and that's our business model."

It's important to note that the oxygen for Zorc's long-term strategy is to keep winning and, at the very least, qualify for Champions League by finishing in the top four of the Bundesliga. If Dortmund isn't in the Champions League, it becomes extremely hard to persuade a top prospect like Dembélé or Guerreiro to choose an offer from BVB over one from Real Madrid, PSG, or any other team in the Champions League. And if Dortmund's performance goes completely down the drain—as it did during Klopp's last season in 2014–15, when the club was near the bottom of the Bundesliga for most of the campaign—then the uncertainty creates a knock-on effect in which players are unwilling to sign long-term contracts and may choose to sign only one-year deals.

Such was the case in the annus horribilis of 2014–15. "All the players got frustrated in this time, and at one point in the season we were last in the table," Zorc recalls. "We lost at home against Augsburg and we were in 18th place. And at this time it wasn't possible for us to get a renewal of the contracts, because the players didn't know what the sporting perspective would be. That's why we had to face a really difficult situation [in the summer of 2016]. It's more about having long contracts than of having contract durations which are year by year."

As a result, Zorc faced one of the toughest decisions of his career in the summer of 2016. Three of Dortmund's best players— centerback Mats Hummels, midfielder Ilkay Gündoğan, and forward Henrikh Mkhitaryan—all had just one season remaining on their contracts. All of them were in demand by some of the world's biggest clubs. All of them were interested in leaving Dortmund. But if Zorc sold them all at the same time, would it cripple BVB's chances of performing well in the 2016–17 season? It was a big risk. "First, none of these players wanted to renew their contracts," Zorc says. "All three players had a contract of one year left, so that means for us selling them now or letting them go for free the next summer. And there was a willingness from each player to leave now. Sometimes a player will say, 'Hey, I will stay and leave the club the next season for free, and I will cash in on the transfer amount [by getting a higher salary due to having no transfer fee].' So this was a very special situation with these highly rated players. In the end we were forced to sell them."

Zorc still marvels at the prices he was able to get for Mkhitaryan (€42 million to Manchester United), Hummels (€35 million to Bayern Munich) and Gündoğan (€27 million to Manchester City). "What we reached was at least a world record," he says, "because no club had ever received more than €100 million for three players who all had one-year contracts left. Maybe this will change in the future if the Chinese continue to buy players for huge amounts, but if there's a one-year contract left, a club can get him next year for free, so normally you'll only get €10 million to €20 million for players in that situation. When Toni Kroos left Bayern Munich for Real Madrid, he had one year left and he was an outstanding player who had just won the World Cup. And Bayern received just €22 million. We received for our three more than €100 million."

Dortmund still needed to perform well in the Champions League and the Bundesliga to keep Zorc's overall strategy going, and, after sustaining the loss of three key veteran players, he sought to minimize the risk as much as possible. "In football there is always risk, so it's about probability," he says. "I was very convinced about the young players we had signed, but we also tried to buy some safe havens." That meant signing established players like André Schürrle (€30 million), Mario Götze (€22 million), Sebastian Rode (€12 million), and Marc Bartra (€8 million) in the summer of 2016, in addition to the youngsters Dembélé (€15 million), Guerreiro (€12 million), Emre Mor (€9.75 million), and Mikel Merino (€3.75 million). The teenagers Christian Pulisic and Felix Passlack, who had been promoted to the first team in early 2016, were like two new signings as well. Ultimately, Zorc's risk paid off: In 2016–17, after losing three of its best players, Dortmund reached the Champions League quarterfinals, won the German Cup, and qualified for the following season's Champions League by finishing third in the Bundesliga. Perhaps the biggest surprise was that the new veterans— Götze, Schürrle, and Rode, all dogged by injuries and subpar performance—provided less to the team than the youngsters Dembélé, Guerreiro, and Pulisic. "In the end," Zorc says, "that convinced us to continue with our strategy to focus on these young promising players."

Underlying Zorc's belief system is a deep and abiding faith that if he loses a key player, he and his staff have the talent and the ability to replace him with another one. "Maybe at a certain point we sell Aubameyang for a high amount," Zorc muses one day in the spring of 2017 about his top striker. "He's now getting toward 28, and maybe it's the last time to get real big money for him, because transfer fees decrease rapidly with the age of the players. If we receive, let's say, €70 million or €80 million, I won't spend it for one player, because we'll try to find the new Aubameyang. That might be nearly impossible at this moment!" He sighs, as though he is convincing himself it would indeed be possible, because he has done it before, from Frei to Barrios to Lewandowski to Aubameyang (and don't forget Mkhitaryan). "But when Lewandowski left, everyone said, 'Who will score for Borussia Dortmund?' And then Aubameyang scored more goals than Robert." (Dortmund eventually sold Aubameyang to Arsenal in January 2018 for €63.8 million.)

Zorc's beloved hometown club, the one he has been part of since 1978, is secure now. There is no danger of bankruptcy anymore. He has refused entreaties from suitors like Arsenal. "I have a long-run contract here and a lot of work to do," he says, "and I like working here at Borussia." Yet there are always challenges.

In August 2017, Bayern Munich tried (and failed) to poach Mislintat, his chief scout, but Arsenal succeeded in doing so a few months later. At the same time, Zorc is starting to sense the generation gap with Dortmund's youngest players. "A big issue is trying to feel how a player feels, to put myself in their shoes," he says. "And that's getting more difficult as you get older. But if you work with young players, as we like to do, I think that's an important issue."

Zorc's strategy is an ever-evolving one, but the core principles remain in place. Invest in the academy. Buy low and sell high. Hire coaches willing to put in the time and develop talented young players. Give those prospects a chance on the field. Play a dynamic brand of soccer. And balance the youth with enough veteran experience to get results, challenge for trophies, and stay in the Champions League. In the modern game, no head coach who's responsible for preparing his team to play two games a week can have the time or the energy to do what Zorc does so well as the sporting director at Borussia Dortmund. The club gave Zorc the freedom to establish his long-term strategy without having to worry that he could lose his job after a three-game losing streak. And even though his staff's scouting of players may not rely much on new-age data analytics, Zorc has shown that you can mix a modern strategy and business model with old-school talent identification. And that in itself is something new.

ACKNOWLEDGMENTS

There are many people to thank. Mary Reynics, my editor at Crown, supported the idea for this book and my ability to do it, displaying remarkable patience as I devoted several years to starting a television career. My agent, Chris Parris-Lamb, has tremendous taste and helped me through the idea-formation process in a macro and micro sense. Special thanks go to Chris Stone, the editorial director for *Sports Illustrated*, who generously gave me a leave of absence for four months to write this book. David Neal, my boss at Fox Sports television, also let me lie low during the summer of 2017 as I wrote this manuscript.

Additionally, I would like to thank the political columnist George Will. In 1990, Will wrote a classic book called *Men at Work: The Craft of Baseball*. He divided baseball into four component functions and picked one person of accomplishment and surpassing intelligence to fill each role. You could apply Will's idea to write a book exploring the craft of any sport, and that's what I have done here with soccer. I would like to think I had as much fun diving into this project as Will did on his book. I'd like to thank the clubs and agents that helped arrange my interviews, as well as the team backroom wizards who put together the video-clip packages that I watched with the players and technical staff. Standouts in this area include Martin Hägele, Vicky Kloss, Simon Heggie, Rob Moore, Matthew Moore, Daniel Stolpe, Dirk Mesch, Brian Doogan, and Tim Scanlan. Thanks also go out to data wizard Ben Torvaney, Gus McNab, and Opta's Oliver Miller-Farrell. The team at Crown has been terrific, including Molly Stern, Annsley Rosner, Tricia Boczkowski, Tammy Blake, Melissa Esner, and Maya Lane.

Most of all, I would like to thank the participants in this project—Xabi Alonso, Javier Hernández, Vincent Kompany, Roberto Martínez, Manuel Neuer, Christian Pulisic, and Michael Zorc—for their time, their knowledge, and their trust. (Juan Carlos Osorio might as well be a full character in the book, too.) European soccer is a punishing sport. The games are constant. The mental and physical demands are exhausting. The vacations are few. Yet these figures all made the time to sit down with me multiple times over two years, to watch hours of video and to answer all my questions, including the stupid ones (sorry, guys!). In different ways, they answered a straightforward query: While all of us see the games on our TV screens or at the stadiums, what's going on in the minds of the players and the managers that informs what's happening in front of us?

The people I chose for this book are exemplars of the modern game. Over the years, in interviews with players and coaches from around the world, it struck me that the old standby cliché for soccer ("the beautiful game") was rarely a phrase that any of the people inside the sport actually used when talking about it. But the phrase "the modern game" would come up all the time. If you ask a thoughtful player what "the modern game" means to him or her, be prepared for an intriguing 10-minute response. But if you ask the same question about "the beautiful game," be prepared for quizzical looks, rolled eyes, and perhaps some vague references to the 1970s. That makes sense. "The beautiful game"—*O jogo bonito* in the Portuguese of Brazil, which coined the phrase—reached its zenith with Brazil's Pelé-led 1970s World Cup champions and lost its relevance inside the sport when Brazil's Sócrates-led 1982 team got knocked out of the World Cup by Italy. That's not to say the figures in this book play artless, ugly soccer. Far from it. Every week they show that they are by turns cerebral and electrifying. But if you see the video of games from today and those of the 1970s, it might as well be a different sport. The modern game, the 21st-century version that we love watching, has been the focus of this book.

Liviu Bird, Shaw Brown, and Brian Straus took the time to read drafts of this book. My deepest thanks go to the people who helped me make a career out of writing: Bambi Wulf, Gloria Emerson, Bill Colson, Peter Carry, Frank Deford, Martin Dale, David Remnick, Landon Jones, Gene Miller, Carlos Forment, Judy Barnes, Jane McCue, Jack Liles, Nora Pinkston, and Judy Dunseth. I am also indebted to the writers, editors, producers, and photographers of *Sports Illustrated*, past and present, especially Jon Wertheim, Alex Wolff, Scott Price, Steve Rushin, Gabriele Marcotti, Simon Bruty, Terry McDonell, Paul Fichtenbaum, Hank Hersch, Adam Duerson, Ryan Hunt, Avi Creditor, Mark Mravic, Greg Kelly, Chris Hunt, Gabe Miller, Maggie Gray,

Mark Bechtel, Lee Feiner, Josh Oshinsky, Steve Cannella, Mark McClusky, Dick Friedman, Sandy Rosenbush, Luke Wahl, and Luis Miguel Echegaray. The gang at Fox Sports has been truly supportive, including Alexi Lalas, Stuart Holden, Rob Stone, Kate Abdo, Landon Donovan, John Strong, Warren Barton, Brad Friedel, Maleek Ndile, Zac Kenworthy, Rachel Bonnetta, Joel Santos, Jen Pransky, Bardia Shah-Rais, Spandan Daftary, John Entz, David Nathanson, Judy Boyd, Jonty Whitehead, Fernando Fiore, Aly Wagner, Keith Costigan, Ben Grossman, Dermot Mc-Quarrie, and Eric Shanks. My deepest appreciation also goes to David Hirshey, Zach Dixon, and David Gernert.

My parents, Helen and David Wahl, gave me a love of sports, and my brother, Eric Wahl, has given me great pleasure as he has become a hardcore soccer fan.

My wife, Céline Gounder, remains a source of inspiration for continuing to do amazing work as a doctor in Ebola-plagued Guinea, opioid-ridden Appalachia, and the lowest life-expectancy areas of the rural United States. More than half of this book was written on her worksite at the Indian Health Service hospital on the White Mountain Apache reservation in Whiteriver, Arizona.

INDEX

ALSO BY GRANT WAHL

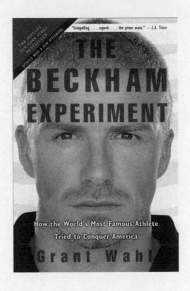

"Compelling . . . a detailed, carefully reported account."

—*Los Angeles Times*

"An engaging peek into the weird worlds of Beckhamania and U.S. soccer. Grant Wahl, the country's best writer on the sport, may even convince all those who played soccer as kids to remember why they loved the game."

—Frank Deford, author of
The Entitled: A Tale of Modern Baseball

THREE RIVERS PRESS
NEW YORK

AVAILABLE WHEREVER BOOKS ARE SOLD